Focus Group Practice

Claudia Puchta and Jonathan Potter

SAGE Publications
Los Angeles • London • New Delhi • Singapore

First published 2004
Reprinted 2006, 2007

SAGE Publications Ltd.
1 Oliver's Yard
55 City Road
London EC1Y 1SP

SAGE Publications Inc
2455 Teller Road
Thousand Oaks, California 91320

SAGE Publications India Pvt Ltd.
B1/I1 Mohan Cooperative Industrial Area
Mathura Road, New Delhi 110 044
India

SAGE Publications Asia-Pacific Pte Ltd
33 Pekin Street #02-01
Far East Square
Singapore 048763

British Library Cataloguing in Publication data
A catalogue record for this book is available from the British Library

ISBN: 978-0-7619-6690-6 (hbk)
ISBN: 978-0-7619-6691-3 (pbk)

Library of Congress Control Number: 2003104419

Typeset by Photoprint, Torquay, Devon
Printed and bound in Great Britain by Athenaeum Press Ltd., Gateshead, Tyne & Wear

Focus Group Practice

Contents

Preface

This book emerged out of collaboration between an active market researcher with many years of practical experience in moderating groups (CP) and an academic social psychologist with many years' experience of analysing people's talk (JP). Its motivation was both the excitement of considering the detail of what goes on when researchers and volunteer participants come together in a focus group, and a feeling that current books on the conduct of focus groups are missing something important.

Although a number of books claim to guide researchers through the task of moderating groups, for the most part they provide little on the moment-by-moment business of bringing the groups to life and managing the various troubles and opportunities that arise. Instead they tend to be too abstract (remember that participants really do have wisdom – which is nice, but hard to act on) or too prosaic (don't forget that crisps make nasty crunching noises on the tape – which is not news to most people). It is not that they are not valuable – they are full of useful lessons; it is that they are incomplete. We have deliberately tried to focus our book on what is left out of the others and, concomitantly, spent less time on general features of moderation, as well as the administrative and planning side of groups which are well handled elsewhere. Our book is unique in concentrating on the interaction itself.

Our collaboration started with CP working on a set of German market research focus groups and trying to apply some of the ideas from conversation analysis and discursive psychology that JP had been developing and drawing on at Loughborough. The success of this research encouraged us to collect a broader set of focus group materials from UK market researchers with a wider range of products and services.

We have looked at what moderators actually do. That is, we used audio and video records to see how they set people at their ease, how they elicit the right kind of information from people, and how they head off unproductive lines of interaction without endangering the relaxed and spontaneous feel of the interaction. Our aim is to capture the skilled practices that good moderators perform smoothly and, seemingly, without thinking about them, and lay them out for study. By understanding what those practices do – how they solve problems, generate kinds of interaction – we hope to help moderators think about their practices in a more strategic manner. If the book has a slogan (doesn't every book now have to have a slogan?) it would be this: *turning practices into strategies*. We would like to help focus group researchers build on their skilled practices in a thoughtful and strategic way. We hope they will gain more insight into what they do well already, and gain some new strategic skills that will make their groups better and more rewarding. At the same time, we will look at some of the things that can go wrong in interaction and how they can be headed off or ameliorated.

We will try to help focus group researchers on two levels. At the most concrete level we will illustrate the working of particular focus group practices such as eliciting information by giving detailed examples from actual groups. At a broader level we will provide information about the general ways interaction works – how conversation is organized, how views are expressed, and how descriptions are built as parts of actions. Our belief is that a general understanding of interaction will help anyone involved in moderating focus groups to better appreciate why focus group participants say, or perhaps don't say, what they do.

We hope a number of different groups of people will find the book useful. Most importantly, we hope that it will be helpful to everyone who is involved in the running, analysis and use of market research focus groups. First and foremost it is a book for them. Indeed, we hope they will recognize their moderating practices and develop a deeper understanding of how and why they work. Our belief, however, is that many of the issues that we address are not restricted to market research groups, but are generic to focus groups across the social sciences. Although there will be some difference in emphasis and use we expect that much of what we document will be recognizable in social science focus groups and those run by political researchers. More generally still, we hope the book will interest people involved in a range of practices where strangers come together for a collaborative but directed task – health support groups, say, or some work consultation groups. Finally, we hope that the book will interest people who are concerned about the ways social science can be applied, as it attempts to show a different way of making work in conversation analysis and discursive psychology useful.

Acknowledgements

We have a range of people to thank who helped us in various ways with the production of this book.

Most importantly we would like to thank the market researchers, advertising agencies and companies in Germany and the UK who kindly provided us with examples of their focus groups on audio and videotape. Without their patience and trust this book would have been impossible. We hope they will appreciate the result.

Parts of Claudia Puchta's work were supported by a grant given to her from the Deutsche Forschungsgemeinschaft, Germany.

At the same time, the book has benefited from input from members of the Loughborough Discourse and Rhetoric Group (DARG). Although it is hard and pick out people who made a particular impact, we would like to name Celia Kitzinger, Derek Edwards, Mick Billig, Sue Wilkinson and Walter Karl as having made special contributions in one way or another. Most important was Sally Wiggins who helped with the practicalities of contacting companies and spent hours improving on our transcripts. Various academics from outside have commented on chapters or related articles and have helped the development of the work. We thank especially Alexa Hepburn, Greg Myers, Nik Coupland, Steve Reicher and Sue Condor. The other person we would single out is Duncan Hepburn. He devoted much time to converting German English to English English, and trying to make our writing more elegant – the remaining grammatical tangles are, of course, our own.

1 Focus Groups and Interaction

The aim of the book

Our aim is to offer a clearer understanding of the practice of focus group moderation. We hope to make more visible what moderators and focus group participants actually do in focus groups. As the reader works through the book we hope they will gain a progressively deeper feel for the intricate way that moderators' activities link in with participants' activities. There is what we would like to call an interactional choreography at work. Good moderators can smoothly perform the steps of this choreography without thinking. Those new to moderation know just how easy it is to tread on the toes of their participants, and just how elusive a really smooth flow of interaction can be. Our hope is that the book will contribute to this skill; it will offer a few dancing lessons, it will show how some of the moves of good dancers are put together, and it will provide some of the resources needed to build new dances.

These features of the book should also appeal to different readers. On the one hand, focus group moderators and market researchers will appreciate practical guidance; on the other, those academics, who are interested in focus groups as a research instrument or in talk per se will appreciate the explication of how groups are managed. In addition, it will contribute to a growing literature that takes research methods as a topic for study in its own right.

How to read this book

This book offers a new approach. Focus group interaction has been neglected for a long time. Although it is widely accepted that the use of focus groups is a research technique that collects data through group interaction (see for example Morgan, 1997), only a small number of focus group researchers recognize this interaction as a resource in data analysis.

The primary emphasis of this book will be on what conversation analysts call talk-in-interaction. They describe talk in this way as they wish to highlight what people actually do with talk rather than the sorts of abstractions about grammar or semantics studied by linguists. For much of the twentieth century an abstract linguistic approach dominated research, and one might have been forgiven for thinking that talk was the second-class citizen of the social science world; something rather rough and ready when compared with the elegance and purity of perfectly formed grammatical sentences. It is only recently that researchers have started to look at what happens when people talk to one another, when they chat or gossip, when they flirt or complain. The beautiful thing here is that what seemed rough and ready turns out to be intricately organized in a way that enables people to get things done. Talk-in-interaction is quite different from talk in the grammar book or talk in the philosophy text; it is bound up with people's lives – their projects, their developing identities, their evaluations.

The success of recent work on talk has come from abandoning many past theoretical assumptions and stipulations about language and instead looking carefully at what is going on. Ironically, the most powerful tradition of research on language in the last 30 years (associated with the linguist Noam Chomsky) virtually ruled out the study of actual talk, on the grounds that it would be too messy to make sense of! The success of work in conversation analysis and discursive psychology has arisen from ignoring such stipulations and going out into the field with tape recorders and video cameras.

We have followed through this approach with the topic of focus groups. Rather than work with theoretical stipulations about what goes on in groups, or with moderators' post hoc reports of what went on, we looked at what is actually said in them. This means that our conclusions will be of a different order to what is found in previous books on moderation. We will develop our understanding of what moderators do without pigeonholing them with general labels such as the seeker of wisdom, the enlightened novice or the therapist. We will also attempt to keep our descriptions of what people do relatively concrete and close to the practices in the groups; we will avoid abstract descriptions of idealized moderator behaviour invoked with terms such as communication skills, interest in people and openness to new ideas. We all know that these qualities are helpful (imagine a moderator who used their poor communication skills to show their lack of interest in people and their resistance to new ideas!). The hard thing is to specify what such qualities amount to in practice.

In addition to these descriptions and suggestions about focus group moderation the book will offer a broader level of help. We believe that it will be useful to focus group moderators to have a general understanding of how interaction works, and in particular how conversation works. Again, we expect that moderators will have great practical skills as talkers – most of us have. But we would like to develop a more explicit and strategic understanding of conversation. To support this we have chosen to break up the text with a serious of boxes that introduce key features of conversation. These inform the observations about focus groups, but they will also provide a general feel for interaction and its features.

These boxes provide another way of reading this book. It can be read as in introduction to interaction using what goes on in focus groups as a major illustration. The boxes can be read without reference to their surroundings – at times they are linked to specific features of focus groups discussed in the text; at times they have only a general relevance. Sometimes they provide a slightly different take on material in the main text. At other times they highlight an important concept or finding from the study of interaction.

This book will be helpful to focus group moderators and social scientists in three specific ways.

- First, it will make specific observations about focus group interaction and how it can be managed.
- Second, it will provide a generic understanding of how interaction works which may help interpret events in groups and suggest new practical exercises for the participants.
- Third, it will be useful for social scientists interested in understanding social science methods and the integration of discursive psychology and conversation analysis.

Transcript and talk in the world

One of the features of this book is that we will work with extracts from actual focus groups run by a range of market researchers involved with big name brands. This is real interaction – not something made up and cleaned up to illustrate how things ought to work, and not something put together from memory and in line with theories and expectations. However, the use of such transcripts presents a dilemma. They are likely to seem unfamiliar at first, cluttered with symbols indicating features of speech delivery and intonation.

We have thought long and hard about cleaning them up by taking material out and thereby simplifying what is shown. But to do this would have been counter to the central theme of the book, which is that the practice of moderation is delivered in the specifics of what is said, and that such specifics are delicately organized. A wealth of research on conversation leads to the inexorable conclusion that *no* detail of interaction can be safely dismissed as insignificant. No facet of speech, whether it is a pause, a repair, a change in pitch or volume, the selection of particular words, the point at which one speaker overlaps another, or even a sniff, should be assumed to be irrelevant to interaction. This is one of the reasons why it is hard to provide *general* rules for what moderators should do. The specifics often override the apparent generalities.

Transcribed talk looks messy, probably much messier than we might expect having grown up with a diet of play scripts, newspaper summaries of conversations, and the kind of idealized representations that are common in instruction books for all sorts of activities, including manuals for running focus groups. But that is what real talk is like. Speakers hesitate, pause, repeat themselves and correct themselves. They can respond to hesitations that are too small to measure with a stopwatch, and capture nuances of intonation that suggest trouble or confusion. As everyday speakers we have enormous practical skills – after all we have spent much of our life practising talking, which is more time than with virtually any other deliberate human activity. It would be surprising if we could not breeze an A = in our advanced speaking exams every time! Yet when it comes to *characterizing* this complexity we are not nearly as skilled. When we try and *describe* it or *explain* it we struggle. These are not things we have to do very often in everyday settings that are overwhelmingly practical rather than theoretical.

We hope that readers will quickly get used to reading the transcript that appears in the following chapters, and thereby develop a feel for the way it captures the spoken quality of interaction over and above the words used. The transcript will help make moderation practices explicit, and start to indicate features of interaction that can be drawn on to make moderation more effective. The transcription system used here was developed by Gail Jefferson over the course of a range of studies starting in the 1960s. It has been tried and tested in conversation analysis and discursive psychology, and has been found to capture much of what is significant in interaction – we will introduce it with an example later in the chapter, and it is reproduced in full in an appendix.

A short history of the focus group

David Morgan (1998) describes the history of the focus group as falling into three periods:

- early work carried out by both academic and applied social scientists;
- market research carried out in the period between the Second World War and about 1980;
- recent research in both academic, market research and political settings where they have been conducted in many different fields.

Social science origins

Merton is considered to be the father of the focus group, and the first example of focus group research is Paul Lazarsfeld's and Robert Merton's work at Columbia University in 1941, when they tested people's reactions to wartime radio broadcasts. After the war, Merton and two of his students,

Patricia Kendall and Marjorie Fiske, wrote an influential book on focus groups that has since been reprinted several times (Merton et al., 1990 [1956]).

Focus groups as an isolated market research method

Between 1950 and 1980 focus groups were rare outside the field of market research. Merton and Lazarsfeld were themselves increasingly drawn to survey-research and away from the focus group, though a direct connection between market research and focus groups was established as Lazarsfeld often used marketing projects in order to finance his academic research. However, the move to marketing was also driven by the uses that market researchers themselves created for focus groups. They frequently referred to focus groups as *group depth interviews* (Goldman et al., 1987). The *depth* in this alternative title marks the involvement of psychoanalytic theory in understanding what is going on, and particularly the hidden, unconscious motives lying behind the consumption of different products.

During this period neither psychology departments nor business schools offered any instruction in the techniques of running and analysing focus groups. Morgan (1998: 40) notes that since few market researchers published descriptions of their focus group technique they failed to have the influence they might have on the development of new procedures and uses for focus groups.

Focus groups as a widespread research method

According to Morgan (1998: 40) applied social research was the vehicle that spread focus groups beyond the world of product marketing. In 1981 Evelyn Folch-Lyon and her colleagues published articles on their efforts to promote the use of contraceptives in Mexico (see for example Folch-Lyon et al., 1981). They used focus groups and surveys to explore knowledge, attitudes and practices concerning contraception among different social groupings in the Mexican population. Another early piece of applied research project was run by Dayle Joseph and colleagues (1984). They constructed a questionnaire that surveyed, with the help of focus groups, the reactions of gay and bisexual men regarding the emerging AIDS epidemic.

Since then focus groups have become increasingly popular as a tool in applied social research, especially in the field of health (see Wilkinson, 1998a for a detailed overview of focus groups in health research). It is also worth noting John Knodel's (1995) work in Thailand on the decline in fertility, attitudes towards prostitution, and the support people give their ageing parents, as well as Charles Basch's work on focus groups as a research technique for improving theory and practice in health education (1987), and (with his colleagues) on the decision-processes of young drivers (1989). In the mid-1990s psychologists and communication researchers Peter Lunt and Sonia Livingstone (1996) started using focus groups to examine how an audience interprets media messages. In the same year focus groups came to prominence in Britain when it was revealed that political parties were employing them as part of their election strategies (Johnson, 1996: 519). Since then focus groups have become synonymous with a particular style of political consultation to the point that they are sometimes accused of driving policy and threatening proper democracy.

In the late 1980s the first book-length text on focus groups by marketers appeared (Goldman et al., 1987) and since then there has been a regular stream of publications on the topic. For social research the most important books are those by David Stewart and Prem Shamdasani (1990), David Morgan (1993), Richard Krueger (1994), Sharon Vaughn and colleagues (1996), Thomas Greenbaum (1998, 2000) and Michael Bloor and colleagues (2001). In 1998 *The Focus Group Kit* was published with volumes by Morgan and Krueger.

For a more detailed history of the focus group, see (among others) Johnson (1996), Vaughn and colleagues (1996) and Morgan (1997, 1998).

What are focus groups?

There is no shortage of definitions of what a focus group is. According to Vaughn and colleagues (1996) it usually contains the two following core elements:

- a trained moderator who sets the stage with prepared questions or an interview guide;
- the goal of eliciting participants' feelings, attitudes and perceptions about a selected topic.

Morgan (1998: 33, 34) draws attention to the abuse of the term 'focus group', there being any number of things which are called focus groups but which fall, according to him, outside the current definition. These groups:

- do not involve research such as support groups;
- are not focused, because the moderator does not or cannot keep the group focused;
- are only *nominal groups*. In nominal groups – described in Stewart and Shamdasani (1990) – participants do not interact with each other, but are interviewed as individuals.

Uses of focus groups

The use of focus groups can be differentiated according to the *desired outcome* and the *type of research question*.

Type of outcome: Focus groups can be self-contained, or can be used as an adjunct to other research methods such as individual interviewing, participant observation, surveys or experiments (see Morgan, 1997 and Wilkinson, 1998a). According to Sue Wilkinson (1998a), the two most common research designs involve the use of focus groups in an initial exploratory or hypothesis-generating phase, and in a final follow-up phase that pursues exploratory aspects of the analysis.

Type of research question: When focus groups are used in the context of marketing, either in profit-making or non-profit organizations, the research is mostly concerned with an evaluation of marketing products and/or services. Examples of this would be focus group studies on the acceptability of new cars (for example Stewart and Shamdasani, 1990: 129–38) or on the evaluation of mental health programmes (for example Richter et al., 1991).

When focus groups are used in the context of health education the research is mostly concerned with the promotion of awareness and the facilitation of behaviour change. Examples of this would be focus group studies on sex education, particularly on the promotion of safer sex in the context of HIV/AIDS (for example Kline et al., 1992) and on the responses to health-related messages (for example Philo et al., 1994).

Focus groups are also used in the context of participatory and action research, with the intent to empower and to foster social change (see Cunningham-Burley et al., 1999, and Johnson, 1996). An example of this is the action research conducted to enable Hispanic students in a community college to overcome barriers to success (Padilla, 1993).

The use of focus groups in marketing research

In an influential paper, Bobby Calder (1977; see also Calder, 1994) describes three different approaches to focus groups – the *exploratory*, the *clinical* and the *phenomenological*. Whereas the exploratory approach seeks to obtain what Calder calls *pre-scientific knowledge* in areas that are relatively unknown to the researcher, the clinical approach seeks *quasi-scientific explanations* (1977: 355) and is based on the premise that the real causes of what people do must be discovered (and can be discovered) through the clinical judgement of trained analysts. However, for us the phenomenological approach is the most relevant as it is the most common in market research.

Marketers usually belong to different social groupings from their target groups, and focus groups are seen as a way of bridging that social gap and *experiencing* a *flesh and blood* consumer (Axelrod, 1975: 6). The logic of the phenomenological approach is that in order to be effective in advising on the marketing of products and services the researcher must share the experience of consumers – she or he must be somehow personally involved with them. Watching the video, or watching through a one-way mirror, should allow the researcher to develop an understanding of how consumers are feeling about the product. Focus groups should allow the researcher to *experience the experiencing of consumers.*

This is where focus groups are crucially different from other kinds of research such as questionnaires or surveys. The findings cannot be neatly summarized in a numerical or even a propositional form. Rather they depend on the way the participants describe and evaluate things. The moderator and researchers develop an understanding through watching and taking part. This emphasis also separates market research focus groups from social science focus groups where the requirements of publication mean that findings have to be made concrete in an explicit propositional form, in claims, descriptions and arguments. Rather than use video and one-way mirror, social science groups depend on publication in books and articles.

Conversation Analysis and Discursive Psychology

We have developed our understanding of what goes on in focus groups using two relatively new perspectives on interaction: Conversation Analysis and Discursive Psychology (sometimes CA and DP). We will need to spend a bit of time describing these perspectives and what they offer. Conversation analysis developed within sociology, discursive psychology within psychology. While conversation analysis shows the virtue of studying interaction between people to help unlock profound questions in sociology, discursive psychology offers a new perspective on basic psychological questions through studying interaction. Both perspectives move from considering unobservable entities out in society or buried in people's heads (things such as social dominance or mental goals) to considering what is directly observable: things that can be seen or heard. The point about things being observable is not a question of scientific adequacy, but comes from considering interaction from the perspective of the people taking part in it. Observability is fundamental to interaction. Why is this?

Say you are entering work and greet a colleague. You say 'hello' and they say 'hi' back. No news there. But what if you say 'hello' and your colleague does not return the greeting? This is more interesting. The first thing to note is what you do not do: you do not think to yourself 'ah well, I must have been wrong about greetings, people don't need to say hello back'. Interaction patterns of this kind are very robust – it would take a lot of failed greeting returns to start questioning them. Instead the failed greeting is an occasion for rich inferences. Did your colleague fail to hear you? Is she upset? Is she angry with you?

The point here is that it is the absence of greeting *just where it would usually (normatively) be expected* that is so clearly observable. These kinds of patterns hold interaction together and, of course, get much more complex than greetings. They are a basic topic in conversation analysis. In this case it is the observable absence of the return greeting that generates psychological speculation about upset or anger. The way that psychology emerges in interaction like this is a basic topic in discursive psychology.

Conversation analysis has been around for about 30 years. It was fashioned in the 1960s by a sociologist called Harvey Sacks. With his colleagues Emmanuel Schegloff and Gail Jefferson he developed a unique approach to conversation and the way it works in interaction. Much of Sacks' classic work was presented in lecture form and it is only in the last few years that its richness has been made more widely available through their publication (as Sacks, 1992). For high quality introductions to conversation analysis see Ian Hutchby and Robin Wooffitt (1998) and Paul ten Have (1999).

Discursive psychology is more recent, being developed out of other areas of psychology in the late 1980s. It draws on and develops the approach to discourse and rhetoric developed by Michael Billig (1996) and Jonathan Potter and Margaret Wetherell (1987). In the last few years it has been established as a major alternative to dominant perspectives in social and cognitive psychology. Derek Edwards (1997) has written a major work contrasting cognitive and discursive psychology; Charles Antaki (1994) has highlighted issues of conflict and argument. For an introduction to discursive psychology see Edwards and Potter (1992).

We will be introducing material from these perspectives in the course of the book as a series of boxes. For the moment we will take a concrete piece of conversation to highlight and further illustrate the way CA and DP approach interaction.

The primacy of everyday conversation

We will focus on an example from a piece of ordinary interaction – a fragment of talk on the phone. Conversation analysts in particular have argued that ordinary talk, mundane talk, the kind of everyday chat we have with one another, is fundamental to understanding all kinds of more specialized interaction. We all spend much of life talking to one another, and talking involves a set of procedures that are both closely and regularly organized and, at the same time, fantastically flexible. Talk is something that we do with intimates as well as strangers, and something we use to perform an enormous variety of the practical tasks of living.

Conversation analysts have shown the way that particular features of everyday talk get modified and developed in institutional settings such as television news interviews, doctors' surgeries and law courts. Our interest, of course, is in the way we can extend this to understanding what goes on in market research focus groups in relation to patterns and activities of mundane interaction. So, here is the example.

Everyday talk in action

Arnold and Lesley are talking on the phone. Do you want to know a bit more about them? Remember, one of the features about interaction emphasized by CA and DP is the way it makes things observable. Features of the relationship between Arnold and Lesley are *displayed* in the inter-action. It shows a degree of intimacy, a degree of prior knowledge and a degree of polite caution. That is what the relationship *is* right here, right now. Are they children, elders or teenagers? We would not start with an assumption that 'youthfulness' is given by chronological age, but again the references to children at college and to parents going on holiday situates them in a broad fashion that is *seeable* in the interaction.

The transcription will seem unfamiliar at first, but it is designed to quickly become intuitive. Emphasis is shown by underlining or colons which mark extensions to the prior sound; changes in intonation are shown by arrows and punctuation symbols. So Arnold's '↑Ye:s.' early in the extract starts with a marked upward intonation but ends with a 'complet-ing' intonation (the full stop here does not mark syntax but an intonational display of having completed an utterance). The first part of the word is emphasized and extended. It may seem a slightly complicated way of showing the sound features of a word, but Arnold is doing something complicated with it. And we will see that such details are fundamental to understanding if focus groups are working well or going wrong. Overlaps are marked by square brackets. Pauses that are short but hearable are shown by a full stop in brackets. Such pauses are less than a fifth of a second, but conversation is so closely co-ordinated that they are clearly hearable. (A full list of transcription symbols and their uses is provided in the appendix).

Lesley has phoned Arnold and is inviting him and his partner out to dinner at a local restaurant.

```
1    Arnold:    We-we were g'nna give you a ring but now you you
2               you've beaten us to ↓i[t!
3    Lesley:                          [eYe:s. Well the ↑children'v
4               all gone back tih college ↓no:w
5    Arnold:    Yes
6    Lesley:    Only just. An:d Gordon and we had t'go to: Kent f'the
```

```
 7              weekend t'see my mother who's going off .t.hhh on
 8              holiday in Canada: an' no:w u-now we're feeling a bit
 9              freer
10  Arnold:    ↑Ye:s.
11  Lesley:    So we wondered if you'd like to meet us
12  Arnold:    Yes certainly.
13  Lesley:    No:w- (0.3) u-we-e m-my hus↑band asked et wo::rk, an'
14              some peh- u-we've never been there.hhhh I, our ↑two
15              local places've gone down hill↓ rather, h-uhm .p.hhh
16              but u-my ↑husband asked et work'n: people said th't
17              the Forge et Chester: Mus↓well was quite good.
18  Arnold:    The Forge:.
19              (.)
20  Lesley:    u-That's ↑quite near you is[n't it.
21  Arnold:                               [Yes it ↑is!
22  Lesley:    Ye[:s.h
23  Arnold:      [↑Ye:s.
24              (.)
25  Lesley:    Ye[s.
26  Arnold:      [It ↑i:s. Ye:[s.
27  Lesley:                  [So: uh we ↑wondered if perhaps we'd.
28              give that a try: what d'you thin:[k
29  Arnold:                                      [What a good idea:.
30  Lesley:    .p.t.hhhhh h-Though we don't know what it's ↓li:ke.
31  Arnold:    No:?
32              (.)
33  Arnold:    W'there's no harm in ↓trying (i[s there).
34  Lesley:                                   [N o : .
```

We will make a series of observations about the extract to illustrate conversation analytic and discursive psychological principles.

Turns, delay and overlap

First, note how little of this conversation is done in overlap; and also how little space there is between Arnold and Lesley's different contributions. People are very attentive to turns of talk and predict very reliably when they will end. Conversation is both very open ended and very predictable. People need to pay close attention to a conversation to take part in it; this is one of the reasons that we get so engaged in conversation.

There is some overlap, but even this is more orderly than it might first appear. Take lines 33 and 34 – Lesley's emphatic 'no' is said over top of Arnold's 'is there'. But note that the 'is there' is not crucial to what Arnold has said; he could quite sensibly finish on 'trying'. This suggests that the overlap is not a result of Lesley failing to pay attention to what is going on, but simply through her making a sensible but wrong prediction of where Arnold's contribution was going to end. Note that the biggest delay in the extract (a huge 0.3 of a second!) is on line 13 – but it is *within* Lesley's turn. She has plainly started to speak, but not yet continued, so Arnold waits.

The general point is obvious, but surprisingly consequential:

> • interaction is organized around turns of talk that are delicately meshed together. It is (typically) smooth and coherent.

This provides a major motivation for all participants in a conversation paying close attention to what is going on. Adding a contribution to an ongoing conversation is a bit like surfing – you have to catch the wave just right otherwise you will just be stuck waiting for the next one.

Actions and adjacency pairs

Talk is *about* things. When we join a conversation we might ask 'what are you talking about?'. Yet talk is also *doing* things. This is often the point of talk; you are saying things to get an enormous range of things done. Let's look at Arnold and Lesley for what they are doing. The core of the interaction is in lines 11 and 12. Put simply, Lesley makes an invitation and Arnold accepts.

Conversation analysts call such activities *adjacency pairs*. This is because in their most standard form the complete activity is done in a pair of turns with the first bit – in this case the invitation – done in one turn and the second bit – in this case the acceptance – done in another. Such pairs are fundamental to interaction. Other examples would be offers and acceptances, requests and acceptances, assessments and agreements, accusations and denials.

Such adjacency pairs bind conversation together. Once the first part has been done, the second part becomes acutely relevant, although other things may need to be sorted out before it is done (this is known as *conditional relevance*). For example, there might have been some sorting out of the scope of the invitation in the extract above before Arnold accepted it, but that sorting out would have all been relevant to the invitation.

The general point is that:

> • actions typically come in adjacency pairs where each part is in a turn of talk contributed by a different speaker.

Actions, delicacy and recipient design

Although the broad pattern seems straightforward enough, there can be a lot of detailed building work that goes into the talk that makes up an adjacency pair. For example, an invitation can be a particularly tricky

Adjacency pairs can be thought of as the basic glue for interaction. Paired actions such as greeting/greeting, invitation/acceptance and question/answer involve close collaboration between two speakers. Getting these things done requires careful attention to one another. Here is a counsellor asking the wife about her marriage in a relationship counselling session.

```
C:      Whe:n:::, (.) before you moved ov↓er here,
        hhow was the marriage.
        (0.4)-
W:      ↑o↓h.
        (0.2)-
W:      I- (.) to me: all alo:ng (.) right up to now, (0.2)
        My marriage was rock solid.
        (from Edwards and Potter, 2001: 19)
```

Note that the 0.4 second delay after the question is asked is very much the wife's delay. The counsellor, the wife and the husband are all orienting to this being a question addressed to the wife, and other business is suspended until that question is addressed.

Adjacency pairs are very powerful. When a question is asked there is a strong orientation to requirement to give an answer. Indeed, if an answer does not arrive immediately this is usually because there are things to sort out (about what the question means, say) before it is delivered. If an answer is not delivered at all this is a noticeable thing and very rich for interaction. If the wife had not answered we might think that she has something to hide. If someone else cuts in before the answer is delivered (say the husband had in the interaction above) then we might wonder why he does not want the answer to be given. These inferences are made possible because of the normative relation between questions and answers.

This normative relationship is very rich psychologically – it provides a machinery for making psychological interpretations (about motive, understanding, opinion and so on). This machinery is inevitably central to focus groups. It allows interaction to take place, and it can be exploited by moderators to generate specific kinds of interaction.

Want to know more?

Excellent introductions to adjacency pairs can be found in Heritage (1984a: 232–92) and Hutchby and Wooffitt (1998: 38–59).

activity to pull off. Note the way that Lesley builds towards the invitation in line 11. She describes various constraints that have been lifted – children have returned to college, mother has been seen before she leaves to go on holiday. This does a number of things.

- First, it describes constraints that explain why the invitation is being offered *now* rather than before.
- Second, the constraints are *family* commitments; that is, they are appropriate and account for the delay in the invitation. They are the sort of commitments kept to by serious caring people, not anything frivolous or trivial. Such commitments typically are treated as taking priority over commitments to other people, for example friends.
- Third, by describing such constraints it implies that an invitation *would* have been offered if the constraint were not there.
- Fourth, by implying that the invitation is being made at the first possible opportunity, the invitation is made to seem well motivated rather than reluctant.
- Fifth, by building up to the invitation with this series of accounts Lesley gives Arnold plenty of warning that an invitation is coming, so he can prepare to respond, because, of course, *turning down* invitations is also a tricky activity.

Conversation analysts term this *recipient design*. In conversation speakers design their talk for the person being spoken to. Again this is not a surprising claim. But its implications for conversational organization, including the conversations going on in focus groups, are profound. To understand what is going on in the first few lines of the extract above we need to see how they are designed to deliver the invitation in a way that attends to Arnold's concerns as a recipient of an invitation.

In general, then:

- actions are built up in a way that is designed for their recipients.

Accountability

We have already noted the delicacy of making invitations. We can see further evidence of this in what Lesley is saying in lines 13 to 17. Lesley is building up to an identification of the venue for the meeting. This involves attending to her *accountability* in making this choice. What makes her choice sensible and justified? Why has she suggested the venue she has suggested?

Note the specific and cautious way that responsibility is assigned – it is not 'we' who asked but 'my husband'. He got a recommendation from others – Lesley herself has no direct experience of the place. The reference to 'two local places' that have 'gone downhill' shows that places where they have eaten in the past are now less good (they are not being kept in reserve for better or closer friends). The point is that choice of venue is very carefully described so that the specific responsibility for the choice is put on the record. Lesley is not directly *accountable* for the quality of the food. Issues of accountability are fundamental to market research focus groups. We will return to them repeatedly in later chapters.

The general point is that:

> • people build the accountability of their decisions, opinions and actions.

Repair

The process of building accounts and descriptions often involves repair. Just like a mechanic fixes the car when it breaks down to make it work, so conversationalists repair their own and, more delicately, other's talk. In this example, we can see Lesley repairing 'we' to 'my husband' at the start of her account for the choice of meeting place. The existence of the repair is one of the ways we see Lesley managing accountability; she fixes the term that may be a problem (the 'we' that included her as a party responsible for choosing the venue) and replaces it with a better one. This piece of talk may seem messy, but if we see it as a building process we can see that it is being assembled and reassembled in a way that best does the business.

In general:

> • repair is a regular feature of conversation, and it is patterned in different ways according to whether speakers are repairing their own talk or, delicately, repairing the talk of others.

Evaluations and assessments

In traditional psychology, evaluation tends to be sited inside people's heads. They have attitudes and opinions to things that they act on or express. Much of the literature using focus groups also takes this kind of position. In contrast, conversation analysis and discursive psychology focus on evaluations and assessments as parts of what people do. And in line with the centrality of observability in interaction, evaluations can be *displayed* in various ways.

We can illustrate this in the extract in two distinct ways. First, we can consider explicit assessments and how they are working in the conversation. Take the description of the restaurant suggested for the meeting. In line 17 the Forge is described as 'quite good'. It sounds like the kind of description that you might put a ring round when you are stopped on Saturday morning in the town centre by an opinion pollster. Yet, before we start to treat this as an opinion residing somewhere in Lesley's head, note that she offered it as a report made by unnamed 'people'. We would be getting into a confused mess if we started treating Lesley as having this view.

More interestingly, 'quite good' works well for the particular business of making this invitation. It is positive enough to be the basis of an invitation (much less and it would be hard to make the invitation seem credible – 'do you want to go to a so-so restaurant we found'!) and yet it is cautious enough that it will not make Lesley responsible if the meal turns out to be poor.

A second illustration of the way assessments figure in interaction is the way conversation is meshed together. Put simply, when speakers start their turns quickly, or even in slight overlap, they can display enthusiasm; while if they delay, even slightly, this can display caution or diffidence. For example, Lesley comes in just a little early on line 3 with an emphasized agreement to Arnold's enthusiasm about contact. More generally, if people follow up an assessment of something with their own agreeing assessment ('the film was lovely', 'yes it was, it fabulous') they often start the turn in slight overlap.

The general points here are that:

- Evaluations may be constructed in particular ways to fit the interaction;
- Evaluations may be displayed by the way turns of talk are organized.

Psychology in action

One of the central themes in discursive psychology is that psychological notions and inner entities have practical things to do in interaction. Rather than our language of psychology being a set of labels for states of mind and the machinery of thinking, they have developed as a toolkit for getting things done: for accusing and excusing; for flirting and teasing.

Part of the key here is the emphasis on observability. Activities work through being visible. Psychology is not so much a hidden thing that lies behind interaction and drives it (an image which most traditional psychologists have worked with, whether psychoanalysts or social cognitivists); rather it is something used *in* interaction and produced *by* interaction.

A piece of interaction like the one above is threaded through with psychological themes, which are built in moments of talk in just the right way to do things. Take the opening contribution from Arnold: 'we-we were g'nna give you a ring but now you you you've beaten us to ↓it!'. He constructs him (and his partner) as having had an intention to phone, and thereby displays a positive attitude to Lesley and the call.

Or take the way Lesley says the invitation: 'we wondered if you'd like to meet us'. She does not make the invitation by directly asking: 'I am hereby inviting you to dinner' (indeed, such directness sounds rather odd). Rather, the invitation is done through reporting something psychological, a wondering about their attitude. In this way she makes it easier to turn down (as in a sense it has not been made, only reported as a wondering). Also, by constructing the invitation in terms of the psychological stance 'liking to meet' up, rather than whether they would actually meet up, Lesley allows Arnold the possibility of displaying the *desire* to meet, but not being actually able to, and constructs the meeting as something that is *wanted* rather than forced. When we look closely at interaction we see that psychology is everywhere; not lying behind it, but in it.

Take one final example. After Lesley's rather complex set of accounts for the quality of the proposed restaurant Arnold repeats the name of the restaurant, The Forge. Repetitions like this are common features of interaction, and they are quite complex. One thing that seems to be going on here is that by repeating the name Arnold shows that he has appreciated which item is crucial. However, repetition can also signal trouble. And indeed, note the way the word is delivered; 'Forge' is extended and emphasized, with a slightly upwards 'continuing' intonation (like an item in a spoken list). So Arnold not only shows he has captured the crucial item, but suggests, indirectly, something more is needed. And note the way that one of the few moments of silence between turns of talk appears just here. This silence is before Lesley comes back with a question about the position of the restaurant. Asking about its nearness neatly suggests a thoughtful, recipient designed, reason for the choice. What counts as common knowledge between these speakers is worked up in the course of these utterances. We will see that conversational phenomena like these are central to interaction in focus groups.

One of the conclusions from discursive psychology, therefore, is that:

- psychological business is attended to in conversation on a number of different levels simultaneously. The psychology is not separable from the interaction itself.

We hope this extended discussion of a single example has illustrated at least some of the main features of conversation analysis and discursive psychology, as well as indicating some of the logic to thinking about interaction in this way. Let us now turn our emphasis back in on focus groups and show how these perspectives can help make sense of what is going on in them.

Focus group talk as task-oriented talk

Focus group moderation is *task-oriented* activity: both moderators and participants *orient to* the task of producing opinions. We use this slightly clumsy term *orient to* deliberately. One of the points we will emphasize

---

Conversation Box 1.2
Talk and action – business is everywhere

Conversation analysts emphasize that action is central to talk. People do not just talk for the sake of it (although it might seem like that at times!) or to give abstract descriptions of the world, but to get things done. Conversation evolved as a medium for action; it is its practical usefulness that gave human beings such a powerful evolutionary advantage. For example, how you describe an object will depend on what you are *doing* with that description. Is it part of a complaint? Is it countering a common expectation or something someone else has said? Is it flirting? Here is the relationship counselling extract from Conversation Box 1.1 again:

```
C:      Whe:n::::, (.) before you moved ov↓er here,
        hhow was the marriage.
        (0.4)-
W:      ↑o↓h.
        (0.2)-
W:      I- (.) to me: all alo:ng (.) right up to now, (0.2)
        My marriage was rock solid.
        (from Edwards and Potter, 2001: 19)
```

The wife is not *merely* answering the counsellor's question; she is answering it in a *particular* way (using certain words and formulations) that counters her husband's version of their marriage as filled with fights and teetering on the edge of breaking up (which, in turn, is related to his justification for an extra-marital affair). When we study what goes on in focus groups we will need to understand it in the context of what Emmanuel Schegloff calls the 'omnirelevance of action'. What group members say, their descriptions and comments, have a rich and detailed organization derived from the specifics of what they are doing.

Want to know more?

Try Wooffitt's (2001) delightful introduction to conversation analysis using the example of psychics. For something a bit more advanced see Heritage (1984a: 150–7) on 'descriptions as actions' or Schegloff (1995).

---

throughout this book is that what is happening in groups is not necessarily thought out, or strategic, or rule following. The task of producing opinions is there in the interaction, and can be quite straightforwardly studied, but the participants are not likely to be thinking about it in this way. We will use the term *orient to* a lot to get away from expectations that people are thinking these things out, calculating and rule following. We do not like to start with these psychological notions as they will quickly take us away from the practical stuff of moderation.

By *orient to*, then, we mean that although focus group members do not necessarily think about what is required of them, they nevertheless tend to provide more in the way of opinions, views, attitudes and beliefs, and fewer stories or personal narratives. With rare exceptions, opinions and views are treated as good contributions to focus groups, and stories or personal narratives are not.

The conversation analysts Ian Hutchby and Robin Wooffitt (1998) distinguish two kinds of task-oriented talk. There is *formal* task-oriented talk, such as that which takes place in courts of law; and there is *non-formal* task-oriented talk, such as appears in GPs' consultations. Formal task-oriented talk involves explicit rules and guidelines; non-formal does not. For the most part, the task orientation in focus groups is non-formal.

Conversation analysts point to the special *inferential frameworks* that arise in task-oriented talk. For example, a professional barrister is unlikely to express sympathy when examining a witness, however sad what is reported. Yet this lack of sympathy will not be treated as unfriendly or callous because of the special inferential framework in the law court. The barrister will be understood as doing her job. In the same way, moderators in focus groups are unlikely to be treated as uncommunicative if they fail to provide their own opinions on products; rather, they will be treated as following task requirements.

In conversation analysis, everyday talk is treated as a benchmark against which other forms of talk-in-interaction can be compared. Task-oriented talk commonly involves a reduction and modification in the range of options when compared with everyday conversation. Comparative analyses of counselling talk, for example, have shown that counselling skills are often embellishments of everyday conversational skills (Silverman, 1997). Whatever the task setting, the point is that mundane skills and understandings are not suspended in favour of something more formal. Rather, people are drawing on their mundane interaction skills, and modifying them to fit the circumstances. For example, the barrister's examination of the witness involves asking questions and the witness gives answers to those questions. In this they are following the formal task orientation. Yet, within this orientation barristers design questions in ways that suggest motivation, criticize conduct and assign blame. This draws on a wide range of mundane interactional skill, little of which is formalized in training.

We will treat focus group moderators in this way. Like the rest of us, they are people who have spent their lives developing a huge and sophisticated native competence in interaction. This is their principal resource in focus group interaction. On top of this, they have developed particular skills in managing focus group interaction. These skills build on their mundane skills. This is not to say that all focus group moderators are equally competent. When watching tapes of focus groups we have been spontaneously delighted by the skills of some moderators, but rather less impressed by others. The point is that moderation cannot easily be separated from the general interaction skills. Our aim will be to make explicit the *unnoticed* skills that moderators employ.

What the book is trying to do: Turning practices into strategies

One principle of this book is to give the moderator control over what she or he is doing in a focus group. That is:

- to make moderation practices more explicit so that they can be used strategically;
- to provide general skills in understanding conversational interaction that can help make sense of focus group interaction.

Both conversation analysis and discursive psychology emphasize that interaction is a flexible, open-ended thing. They understand conduct as non-mechanistic and non-deterministic. People may, or may not, act in accordance with certain conventions. People can make things different. Interaction is full of options and these options are taken up in different ways meaning that it is fluid and creative. CA and DP both highlight the order to this fluidity.

The suggestions we will make in our book will reflect this fluidity and creativity. We will not attempt to give *recipes*; instead we will offer suggestions. We will offer some ways of thinking about what is going on, and how moderators can influence it, that can be drawn on in different ways to improve the conduct of focus groups. We will try and make explicit some of the things that moderators do without thinking so that they can be done more strategically.

Before we outline the book's general themes, though, we must focus on two further points: the social psychological inheritance of focus groups, and the present work's application to market-research and social-science focus groups.

The social psychological inheritance of focus groups and its burden

Much of the conduct of current market research focus groups reflects a legacy of social psychological notions that dates back to the 1950s and beyond. A central idea in this traditional social psychology is the concept of *attitude*. So we can illustrate what is distinctive about our approach by contrasting the traditional social psychological and the discursive approach to attitudes. In traditional social psychology attitudes are seen as having a number of core features:

- they are located within the individual where they are subjectively experienced;
- they can be observed in verbal, behavioural or physiological reactions;
- they are (generally) static;
- individuals differ regarding their evaluative reactions; and
- these reactions can be measured by attitude scales.

This traditional notion has been reworked from a discourse and rhetorical perspective. The rhetorical nature of attitudes is stressed by Michael Billig (1991) who claims that, rather than carry attitudes around as fixed entities, people:

- give views in particular contexts;
- produce evaluations where there is at least the possibility of argument (they tend not to argue about the virtues of gravitational force);
- when expressing an evaluation for something and justifying their own position, people are often criticizing the counter-position.

Billig's argument, then, is that attitudes are inextricable from the arguments in which they occur.

Potter and Wetherell (1987; also Potter, 1998a) have complemented this insight by emphasizing what people are *doing* by making evaluations. They stress that evaluations are not ready-made cognitive objects, but people work up evaluations in ways that are suitable for what is being done. You fashion your evaluation for whether you are making a compliment or a complaint; for whether you are persuading people against a course of action or encouraging them to do something. This discursive psychological approach to evaluation suggests that attitudes are *performed* rather than *preformed*. Moreover, Potter and Wetherell emphasize that in everyday interaction it is often not possible to separate the object from the evaluation. Contrast 'I don't like the feel of this shampoo' with 'this shampoo is very thin feeling'. In the latter case, there is no separate evaluative term, rather we need to work out from the context that the description 'very thin feeling' is part of an evaluation. One of the neat things in everyday talk is that evaluations can be disguised as descriptions; you can be just saying how things are, not offering an opinion in any way.

Our particular interest is in the way the traditional social psychological view of attitudes causes trouble when we try and understand what is going on in focus groups. We will try and show how the discursive alternative gives us better purchase on how they are working.

When attitudes are assumed to be located within the individual, and when such internal states are supposed to be observable in verbal, behavioural or physiological reactions, and when they are regarded as being generally static, it is natural to hope for an effective means of access to these internal states. Traditionally focus groups have been thought to provide this: they were intended to provide a relaxed group setting which will draw out people's opinions and perceptions. The group environment encourages disclosure by providing a degree of anonymity. There is not the same individual focus as with a one-on-one interview. In addition, many researchers argued that focus groups produce data that are rich in detail and would be difficult to achieve using methods such as individual interviews or observation.

However, group dynamics seem to be something of a double-edged sword. When they come to analyse focus group data, researchers tend to view the *group effect* solely in negative terms, as a threat to the authenticity of individual participants' views and experiences. Researchers comment on how difficult it is to separate the views of individuals from those of the group, and speak of the *contamination* of the individual's true response. There is a tension, then, between the benefits of group interaction in encouraging information disclosure, and the danger that it will distort people's expression of their true opinions.

From our perspective these problems are partly a consequence of focus group's social psychology inheritance – the result of conceiving of attitudes as ready-made entities. When we look at focus groups from a discursive perspective, and when we consider attitudes not as *pre*formed but as *per*formed, we no longer need to concern ourselves with the problem of whether individuals are accurately reporting their unique, private, inner attitude, for this is seen as an incoherent notion. For us, attitudes are a product in the social science supermarket that is well past its sell by date! The problem for market researchers is working out how they can give a proper account of phenomena in focus groups without the term.

We no longer need to ask who can or who will provide comprehensive, honest and accurate information about their mental states; and we can stop worrying about whether focus group interaction might distort an individual's true feelings. From our discursive perspective, we are moving from attitudes to evaluative practices that are interesting in their own right. Focus groups provide a setting for developing evaluations in interaction; and that is precisely where evaluations appear in everyday life: in conversation with others, in arguments, embedded in suggestions. We will come back to this topic in the final chapter when we review the book's main findings and draw conclusions from them.

Market research focus groups versus social science focus groups

Focus group interaction, whether for market research or social science, is not *natural* conversation. Few natural conversations focus on a single topic for such a sustained period of time under the direction, whether active or passive, of a moderator. However, the focus group is an event that participants generally enjoy, regardless of whether the topic of discussion is what Miriam Catterall and Pauline Maclaran (1997) would call low-involvement (e.g. what shape is ideal for soft drinks bottles?) or high-involvement (e.g. how should breast cancer awareness be promoted?).

There are also differences between market research and social science research focus groups. Catterall and Maclaran (1997) note that market researchers are reluctant to deal with focus group materials by counting and coding words or opinions and tend not to use computers to aid analysis.

We will see another distinctive feature of market research focus groups in chapters to come: moderators tend to place more emphasis on avoiding contamination from group interaction and on producing non-rational responses. This probably comes from the common marketing presumption that people buy things because of unconscious images and metaphors, irrational associations, and gut feelings rather than more rational considerations.

Although we have emphasized these differences, we will suggest that many of the ideas we will put forward about focus group moderation will apply equally to market research and social science focus groups.

A survey of the book

The book is organized to make clear the range of different tasks the moderator has to accomplish. For the most part these tasks overlap rather than being discrete, but for clarity we have tried to separate them out as far as possible. Each of the chapters ends with a full summary and a set of practical suggestions. These can provide a guide to detailed chapter content for those who want to work backwards. As far as possible the ideas are illustrated with rich examples from actual focus groups.

In Chapter 2 the main issue is the way the moderator can make the focus group informal and relaxed, while managing to keep control over what goes on. How do you make people relaxed? It considers techniques that generate informality and facilitate the kind of interaction that is required. Informality is constructed in the group introduction, it is managed through invoking particular psychological notions, and is a product of particular styles of asking questions.

In Chapter 3 we consider the way groups are organized to encourage participation. How do you get people to talk? The main tool here is the use of a combination of elaborate and simple questions. Elaborate questions are built from a range of different elements – each has a role in encouraging group members to participate. Simple questions are, well, simple.

Chapter 4 concentrates on the production of opinions. How do you get people to give their opinions? In fact, part of the issue this chapter addresses is what kind of thing an opinion is when understood in terms of interaction. The suggestion will be that focus groups can encourage participants to offer evaluations, but also to offer descriptions. Both of these things can be useful. A typical focus group will combine both. Each have their strengths and weaknesses.

In Chapter 5 the concern is with producing the right kind of opinions and avoiding the wrong kind of talk. How do you get people to say the right thing and not the wrong thing? It considers a number of specific techniques. These include the building of candidate answers into questions, requesting descriptions and using repeats to guide responding. It also considers the use of whiteboards and projective questions.

Chapter 6 is about the way a variety of different opinions is produced. How do you get people to give a range of different views? How do you discourage group members from simply agreeing with whatever previous contribution was made? It offers ways in which evaluative questions can be used to generate variety and ways in which descriptive questions can be used to the same end. It also considers some of the difficulties that confront a moderator when they attempt to generate variety.

In the final chapter a number of big issues will be addressed. These include issues of competence and training; the relationship between focus group practice and technical theories from social psychology and psychoanalysis; issues about deception and manipulation; the difference between social science and market research focus groups. It will end with some discussion of technical developments and experiments in new group practice, and what research might lie beyond focus groups.

2 Producing Informality

In our ordinary lives we tend to think of formality as something we have to work at. We learn to stay quiet at the right places in weddings and political meetings, and to pronounce our words carefully and slowly when accepting school prizes. It is easy to think of *in*formality as simply the absence of formality, as a natural state that we settle back into when public pressures are removed. However, those researchers who have looked carefully at interaction have shown that it is not as simple as this. Just like formality, informality often has to be worked at. And one of the paradoxes of interaction is that in formal settings a lot of the work is needed precisely to generate informality. We talk about putting people at their ease and producing a relaxed atmosphere. Skilled moderators know that this is an essential feature of good focus groups.

What we intend to do in this chapter is look carefully at some of the subtle ways that relaxed informality is achieved. Although we tend to think of this as an atmosphere that floats around interaction it is much more than that. In the first place, informality encourages interaction to happen. And, of course, getting people to say something is an absolute prerequisite of group research. More than that, informality facilitates styles of response that are especially useful in focus group work.

In this chapter we will first highlight some general features of the way conversation works, and how psychology appears in interaction, to help us understand what is specific about informality. Then we will break informality down into a number of features with the aim of showing how each can be produced by skilled moderation. In passing, we should note that although our observations are relevant to many different styles of focus groups, they will be less relevant to *nominal* groups or *Delphi* groups in which each participant is asked for their contribution in turn, giving a pattern like a series of one-to-one interviews.

The business

The business of talking

Talking is an activity, certainly. But so are walking or snoring; we mean something more than that by the word business. Talking can achieve something: when a teacher asks a pupil a question, she expects that it will elicit an answer, even if it turns out to not be very informative. But the word business suggests something more than that too. What we have in mind is the work which is being done by *what* we say, the *way* we say it and *when* we say it. The average British adult has a working vocabulary of more than 60,000 words. And this is just the basic raw material for conversation – when these words are used they are put together in ways that transform and inflect their senses. Moreover, when they are used they are not just the flat words in a dictionary – they are voiced. They are delivered with stress and intonation; we can say things with a smiley voice, even with laughter introduced through the words, or we can say things seriously or sadly. The delivery of words indirectly signals information about gender, class and regional identity. When we phone computer support we can be pleasantly surprised to be speaking to a woman with a soft southern Irish accent.

So when we talk of the business of talking we mean the business of the person assembling a contribution to interaction from these various materials, combining together just the right terms, giving them the right intonation and delivery. And we also mean the way the next speaker treats the finessed production of talk that has come before as a basis for what they are going to say next.

The business of being

One simple way of looking at interaction is that there are some people and they are talking. It is so simple that it sounds self-evident. In the traditional social psychology that is taken for granted in much focus group research the nature of self and characteristics such as attitudes are treated as relatively stable properties of individuals. People are ready formed and come together to interact.

Yet, one of the things about conversation is that the people doing the talking do not stand outside of the conversation. They are inside it. Moreover, in interesting and important ways, they are produced by it. Take attitudes for example. In traditional social psychology attitudes are generally treated as static, and are seen as being located within the individual. People come to interaction with an inventory of currently operational attitudes: they think Mars Bars are delicious, conservative politicians are boring, and WAP phones are history. Yet work in discursive psychology by Michael Billig, Margaret Wetherell and ourselves has shown this view to be too limited (Billig, 1996; Potter, 1998a; Potter and Wetherell, 1987; Puchta and Potter, 2002).

This work emphasizes that people develop evaluations when they are performing actions in particular settings. This explains why people's evaluations are often highly variable from conversation to conversation; they vary because the people doing the talking are doing different things with the evaluations. They may say one thing when complimenting, another when complaining, another when persuading someone against a course of action and so on.

Think back to our meal invitation in the last chapter. We noted the way the evaluation 'quite good' was designed to make the invitation work but not generate later problems. In fact, from this perspective the clumsiest thing for interaction would be to have a ready-made cognitive object called an attitude that is wheeled on irrespective of the particular business at hand. The quality of a restaurant will be differently described when we are inviting a new partner to go there, or persuading our mother, or we are suggesting a venue for the office party. The way our description is assembled will relate to the prior expectations of the person invited and the potential upshot of a successful or troubling meal.

It is not just the mental furniture that gets moved around and reshaped in interaction; the whole house gets changed! The identity of the speaker is managed and reworked as people converse. People's talk is put together to present themselves as clever or naïve, mysterious or ordinary. Again, the fundamental issue is what people are doing with their talk. Identities get varied according to the business being done. For example, we might imagine that mostly we would like to appear extraordinary or clever or imaginative. But there are situations where you really want to appear ordinary.

Robin Wooffitt (1992) studied the way people tell stories about paranormal experiences – seeing ghosts or flying saucers; being spoken to by dead relatives. One of the features of the way people tell such stories is that they present themselves as ordinary people. It is not hard to see why. The danger when you tell a story like this is being taken as a crank or mad person; the more ordinariness is emphasized the less likely this is to happen. And you do not want this ordinariness to be spelled out as an obvious attempt to look ordinary, as that might backfire; you want ordinariness to be implied by the organization of what you say. What this example shows is not that the speaker is actually ordinary, or that they are actually anything; rather 'ordinary person' is an identity speakers produce by talking in particular ways. Producing an identity is another part of the business of talking. And it is something we will need to consider when considering focus group interaction, and in particular when we consider how its informality is produced.

Formality and informality

Understanding formality

Formality is characteristic of a range of formal settings – speeches, prize giving ceremonies, courtrooms, parliamentary debates, and so on. Typically formality involves the suspension of everyday patterns of conversational turn taking. When the Vice Chancellor gives his degree day speech you do not feel it appropriate to jump in when he pauses for breath and add an observation of your own: 'that reminds me of the time . . .'. Everyone would turn to frown at you! The next conversational slot is probably the one where the prize recipient says a modest thank you.

Formality is not just an aura, a stiffness that comes from formal clothes or imposing surroundings. Rather, it is specifiable in the way the turn organization of interaction is restricted, both in the pattern of turns and what turns are appropriate. In courts turns are typically required to be, at least minimally, questions and answers. As Max Atkinson and Paul Drew (1979) showed in their study of courtroom interaction, although lots of complicated business gets done when the counsel or barrister interacts with the witness, this business is packaged inside question and answer turns.

Formality is not just there randomly. These sorts of restrictions are there to get business done; if everyone from a large audience added their contributions to the Vice Chancellor's speech just when they wished it would cause all manner of problems. The event would start to become impossibly long, all sorts of problems of seeing and hearing would arise because of the way the seating is organized, several speakers might join in simultaneously (given the way completions are predictable), and there would be issues over precisely who would speak. The restrictions that we gloss as formality are there to get the specific business of degree awarding done.

For us the interest is in focus groups. And here there is a complex set of issues to do with formality and informality. Focus groups are not slices of mundane conversation picked out in conveniently recordable form. They require the participants to give certain types of contribution, and they require the interaction to be organized in certain ways. In this sense, they are situations of formal interaction. Yet, within a range of parameters that we will explore shortly, moderators attempt to generate a situation where interaction seems fluid and spontaneous.

There is a real tension here, which is one of the toughest things to manage when first running focus groups. How can participants be encouraged to make the right sorts of contributions, at the right time, while being relaxed and spontaneous? This is a basic dilemma.

And there is a further issue that this dilemma highlights. As focus groups are a special kind of institutional interaction, the participants are unlikely to come to it knowing what to do. As the conversation analyst Harvey Sacks emphasized, one of the features of social organizations is that they are designed to be learnable. This is a two-way process; people are good at learning how to interact in new sorts of situations; and situations are designed to make their learning straightforward. So another feature we will consider is how participants get socialized into being good focus group participants in various ways.

> **Conversation Box 2.1**
> **The role of formality**
>
> Formality is a characteristic of a range of public, institutional and, well, *formal* settings. Max Atkinson quotes from a Vice Chancellor's degree ceremony speech:
>
> ```
> Speaker    It is (1.0) my very great pleasure (1.0)
>            to welcome you all to this ceremony (1.5) This
>            is the eighth (1.0) of twelve (1.0) Open
>            University (.5) degree ceremonies to be held
>            in nineteen seventy-eight.
>            (from Atkinson, 1982:90)
> ```
>
> Talk like this is distinguishable from informal conversation in a number of ways. There are more frequent and longer pauses within turns, gaps between turns will be longer, there will be relatively few hesitations, hitches and self corrections. This is not just stiffness. Atkinson suggests that formal talk of this kind is functional in the way it manages the interactional problems that arise in settings with large numbers of speakers who do not have a clear view of one another and are unlikely to have their own turn of talk. This means that the pressure to engage in continuous and close monitoring of others is greatly reduced. The participants are unlikely to need to display understanding of what is being said through the timing and design of their own turns. In this kind of situation attention can drift. Features of formality are designed to work against this inattentiveness. For example, the organization of the talk, its volume, its pace, its segmentation through within turn pauses all contribute to making it clear in this environment.
>
> The art in focus groups is to work with the practical emphasis on clarity and shared attention, but against some of the stiffer features of interaction in formal settings.
>
> **Want to know more?**
>
> Atkinson's (1982) is the classic paper on formality, and he developed these ideas more recently (Atkinson, 1992).

Let's start looking at this process of socialization and considering in particular how the tension between making appropriate contributions and being spontaneous is managed.

Producing informality in focus groups

Informality and focus group goals

Focus groups are designed to produce particular outcomes. Unlike everyday talk over dinner it matters greatly to the research what the conversationalists say. However interesting or entertaining, many of the things said over dinner would simply not be relevant to market research questions. It is not just a matter of people drifting off the topic (be it the colour of car seats, or the qualities of a new shampoo) – although that is a problem to be managed. Rather, it is that they could use up the group time with qualifications and disclaimers. Take the following invented example.

Group member	I'm no expert, and I'm not really sure what to say here. I find it really hard to make up my mind. Give me a couple of seconds to consider the ad's pros and cons. It's a bit soon to make a judgement. I mean I'm not really familiar with thinking in this way. I don't usually spend time thinking about margarine ads. But, okay, there is something about the ad I don't like. I'm still not confident in saying what it is though. It's just a vague feeling.

This example is invented, but is meant to bring into being the moderator's nightmare. The speaker is elaborately hedging what they say, they are emphasizing how difficult the task is, how they are not used to doing it, and ending up neither giving a clear evaluation of the ad nor a reason for the evaluation they do give. It is no accident that we had to make this example up – this is one of things that moderators spend a lot of work heading off. All of our materials are from established market research organizations where a lot of moderator effort goes into avoiding this kind of thing.

We will call this kind of talk *account clutter*. It is clutter because it clutters up the interaction with stuff that is, mostly, not useful for the research task. As we will see in the next chapter, however, there are some accounts that are central to focus groups. We thus reserve the term account clutter for hedges, qualifications, expressions of doubt and so on.

Some features of this example probably strike us as rather like what is said in formal settings such as courts and job interviews. One of the features of such contexts is that you are going *on the record*. What you say is the subject of permanent record, and later on you can be identified as the person who said it, who expressed such-and-such an opinion. When you get married the promise to love, honour and obey made on a certain day in a certain place is not (usually!) a spontaneous conversational contribution. Indeed, it is pretty hard to casually get married to people in the course of dinner! Talk in formal settings is often subject to an on-the-record accountability. This can take different forms. Some sorts of accounts are positively useful for focus groups as we will show below. However, what we are considering here are the various hedges and justifications illustrated in the above example, along with its general caution, to highlight how far interaction can become swamped by this focus on dealing with the grounds for making claims. One of the tasks of focus group moderation is to soften this pressure to be cautious about making claims and to surround them with qualifications. We will see moderators using various procedures to counter pressures towards formality.

This generates one of the tensions that lies at the heart of a focus group. On the one hand, moderators need participants to go 'on the record' without worrying that they will be held accountable for their contributions. On the other, they need to be prevented from drifting into informal chatting and personal anecdotes. Managing this tension effectively is one of the arts to running an effective focus group. By lessening the emphasis on accountability participants can be encouraged to produce stronger claims with less hedging. The fundamental task here is how to get participants to produce strong claims that are not swamped by hedging. How can participants be absolved of responsibility for their contributions? At the same time, how can the group be protected against the risks of too much informality? How can people be discouraged from drifting off topic and spending the time telling chatty personal anecdotes?

It's a tough job. Let's look at some of the ways in which it is done.

Working against formality

Let us start with an example. There is nothing better than a real introduction to a real focus group to show some of the complexity of this topic. The following is from a focus group conducted in Germany by a large company. We have tried to capture its texture in the translation. Note a couple of things about our presentation here. As with other extracts from now on, we include relevant information from the video in the right hand column. Sometimes we mark more precisely the appearance of things such as smiley voice by putting asterisks for their start and finish in the main text.

```
M: Brown      And, (.), well, (4.2) ((groans)) We'll er
              make a start, perhaps there'll be, (.)
              someone else along in the, (.7) next five
              or six minutes, (1.2) and, (.) they'll be        participants
              allowed, to take part in this illustrious         cough and
              circle of ours,                                   clear throats
              *otherwise,* (.9) u:h. (.8)                       smiley voice
              First of all my heartfelt thanks, (.8)
              that you're, (.) here and that despite all
              the traffic, (.) you've, (.7) actually
              suc↓ceeded, (.) *in getting here.*                smiley voice
              U:m, (1.7) my name is >Brown like the             moderator and
              colour,< (1.2) and, uh, I uh- now want to,        members smile
              (.) pester the living daylights out of you
```

<table>
<tr><td></td><td>a bit, in the hope, that you, (.9) will
answer as spontaneously as possible, (.8)
there's no wrong answer, there's also no
right answer. It's *just, (.) to find
out, (.8) what your gut reactions are, or*
what you feel or what you think, you know,
(.) uh everybody thinks about the things
in life *in a different way, has,* things
we're talking about, (.8) because of that,
(.) it's not like in school or anything
like that, (.8) and, (1.0)</td><td>moves hand
circling away
from torso

smiley voice

clears throat</td></tr>
<tr><td>Peter</td><td>((clears throat))</td><td></td></tr>
<tr><td>Isa</td><td>Orange juice?</td><td></td></tr>
<tr><td>Ron</td><td>It's alright, thank you,
[(xxxxx)   ]</td><td></td></tr>
<tr><td>M: Brown</td><td>[Yes, (.) you can] of course, (.8) help
yourself as you wish, (.) to all these
things, (.) around you,</td><td></td></tr>
<tr><td>Maureen</td><td>°Thanks°</td><td></td></tr>
<tr><td>M: Brown</td><td>food and drinks. (1.2)
U:h, =we're also ↑taping this, so that I
don't have to write everything down,
because, (.6) uhuh, (.) with my, (.)
scribble it would be a little *difficult,
°to read, (.) it all again afterwards,°*
(.) but perhaps you could tell me a little
bit about, (.) yourselves, before we get
to grips with with the topic, (1.0) about
how old you are, what kind of a job you do
and, *(.8) so on,*</td><td>

smiley voice

turns to
Maureen</td></tr>
</table>

The openings of focus groups vary considerably, and different moderators have different ways of starting them off. However, the example above has many of the characteristics that appear in other groups. Let us pick out some of the features of this opening that help in the production of disciplined informality. We will focus on seven different features of the way informality is produced that involve:

- formulating the nature of the interaction;
- formulating what the interaction is not;
- formulating the psychology of the participants;
- displaying informality through pauses and hesitations;
- displaying informality through word choices;
- displaying informality through intonation;
- managing informality through the physical setting.

1   FORMULATING THE NATURE OF THE INTERACTION

It might be thought that **the most** straightforward way of guiding participants to act in the required manner is to tell them how to act. Group
members could be instructed to be informal but follow the requirements. It
is noticeable, however, that relatively little explicit guidance of this kind is
offered. Perhaps it would be like your dentist telling you to 'just relax'
before starting to drill; some instructions can be counterproductive.
Instead, what tends to happen is that moderators work with what the
conversation analyst Harvey Sacks (1992) called *cover-identities*. The moderator in the passage above sets up a rationale for the forthcoming
interaction as *talk* ('things we're talking about'). Here are a couple more
examples from different groups:

```
And=uh, (.) >we'll then< simply ↑talk ↓about it, (.8)
nothing more and nothing less.

I think, (.) we want to have a ↓chat today about, (.)
shampoos, (.) >I think,< .
```

What is noticeable is that the moderators are not explicitly saying that this
or that will happen in market research focus groups; rather they are
formulating what will go on as talk or even as chat. This is not, of course,
deceptive. None of the participants is likely to be wondering if they went to
the wrong building and ended up having a casual snack with friends.
However, moderators set up talking or chatting as the way to understand
what is going on. They are *euphemisms* of course. From the moderator's
point of view the aim is for 90 minutes of carefully controlled and clearly
videotaped interaction which allows unique access to the members' thinking about a product or service.

In general the focus group topic is alluded to rather than spelled out.
Here is another excerpt from an introduction:

```
I think, (.) we want to have a ↓chat today about, (.) body lotion,
(.) >I think,<
```

Moderators thus promote what is going on as a piece of ordinary, relaxed
and friendly *chat*, as something which is not dry, not very focused, not
task-oriented – almost as if they were to say: 'Don't think that I'm only
interested in your thoughts about cars, shampoo or soft drinks. My interest
in you is much broader!' As Charles Antaki (2000) has shown, the term
'chat' can be used to do some neat rhetorical business.

Instructively, the closest we have found moderators get to being explicit
about focus group motivation is in examples such as the one from the main

extract above where the moderator says he is going to be 'pestering the living daylights' out of participants. Formulations like this display their ironic nature through their extremity (Edwards, 2000); and even here are inexplicit about what this 'pestering' is going to focus on.

2   FORMULATING WHAT THE INTERACTION IS NOT

Although moderators tend to be rather indirect and euphemistic when they are formulating the nature of the focus group, they are very happy to offer elaborate claims about what the group is *not*. For example, in the opening above we see the moderator emphasizing that:

```
there's no wrong answer, there's also no right answer.
```

This is backed up by making a specific contrast between what is going to happen in the group and what would happen in school:

```
it's not like in school or anything like that.
```

This is neat as it sets up a contrast with a situation where people are regularly evaluated. It heads off a specific concern that participants might have. Such explicit formulations are working against the sorts of concerns with accountability that are common in formal settings. It is worth remembering that the focus on informality is intended to have specific outcomes. One of these is to discourage participants from producing the sorts of account clutter that we highlighted in our made up example above.

3   FORMULATING THE PSYCHOLOGY OF THE PARTICIPANTS

Another way of discouraging participants from being concerned with the accountability for their contributions is to construct the psychology of what is required in particular ways. In our focus group opening this is vividly done through the moderator saying he is after 'gut reactions', a metaphor he fleshes out with an expansive hand gesture, and then elaborates as 'what you feel or what you think'.

It is tempting to immediately think of 'gut reactions' and 'feelings' as self-evidently what focus groups are after. However, it is worth thinking about the value of these things a bit more carefully. Objects such as 'gut reactions' and 'feelings' have an immediate virtue in focus groups which is related to their use in interaction as much as their value in market research theory. Specifically, they are objects that require little or no justification. When someone says that they have a 'gut reaction' they are often precisely saying that they are making a claim for which they cannot give an explicit justification. Likewise with a 'feeling' – in our everyday talk feelings are typically contrasted to more rational judgements or factual claims. Unlike more formal knowledge, then, 'gut reactions' and 'feelings' are hard to challenge. By encouraging focus group participants to provide these kinds of psychological objects they are being discouraged from filling their talk with account clutter.

'Gut reactions' and 'feelings' have another feature that makes them ideal for focus groups. They are things that happen to you; they are immediate and responsive. You don't need to figure them out in elaborate ways. They are ideal psychological objects for rapid and fluid interaction. They are the sorts of objects that you ought to be able to produce immediately. Indeed, it is possible that you would be in more trouble if you did not produce your 'gut reaction' immediately. It might suggest that you are embarrassed about it or hiding it for some reason. This provides an added pressure to immediate responding.

A final point to note about the way psychological objects are built in focus groups is the way moderators attend to another potential issue of accountability. Participants might be concerned that reactions and feelings should be relatively standard or shared. This would cause problems in group settings where other members have already offered reactions. A common way of attending to this problem is to emphasize difference. Take the following:

```
uh everybody thinks about the things in life in a different way
```

This has the twin virtues of promoting variation in contributions (if everyone thinks in different ways what you say is unlikely to be just what the last person said) and in discouraging members from taking prior responses as a template for what they ought to say. We will come back to the psychological notions that are the currency of focus groups in Chapter 3 on producing opinions and in Chapter 4 on producing useful opinions, and we will return to issues of variation in Chapter 6. For the moment, the point is the way these notions contribute to the informality of focus groups, and against stilted, cautious, hedged interaction.

4   DISPLAYING INFORMALITY THROUGH PAUSES AND HESITATIONS

One of the principle ways of generating informality is through a particular *style* of talk. If we think of talk in formal situations such as political speeches, courtroom summations and sermons, there are easily recognizable characteristics of delivery. It is often emphatic, evenly paced and loud. Often this talk sounds rehearsed or recited, as if it were the performance of a prior script. Indeed, that is often precisely what it is. What this suggests is that to promote informality in focus groups what is needed is to break up these formal patterns. The inclusion of pauses and hesitations is one way of doing this.

It is important to emphasize that it is not pauses per se that indicate informality. In formal settings talk often includes some delay before particularly important words. Such pauses seem to reduce the risk of hesitancy or of saying something that might require subsequent correction. By including pauses, speakers in formal settings display their concern for precision. The pattern of moderator pauses we see in focus groups deviates from this in interesting ways. Note the way in the following the longish pauses are not placed before key words such as 'answer', 'spontaneously' or 'wrong' as might be expected in a more formal setting:

```
you, (.9) will answer as spontaneously as possible.
(.8) there's no wrong answer
```

The effect of this style of vocal delivery (which is not easy to capture vividly on written transcript) is to present the speaker as improvising. The hesitancy suggests they are searching for words as they go along rather than pausing for emphasis. The suggestion is of spontaneity, which is what is being asked of the participants.

5 DISPLAYING INFORMALITY THROUGH WORD CHOICES

Pauses and hesitations are not the only way to convey casualness: word choices also play a part. Of course, all talk depends on word choice. However, there are types of words that connote particular *types* of inter-action. Linguists talk of words being parts of particular *registers*. There is a register for scientific articles, for example, and another for talking to babies. They are distinct and highly recognizable ways of speaking. Focus group moderators draw heavily on words that are uncommon in the formal registers of ceremonies, courtrooms and so on. They often use language that is rich in metaphor and idiom. In this way they further emphasize the informality of what is going on and contrast it to more formal settings.

In the opening reproduced above, for example, we have 'illustrious circle', 'pester the living daylights', 'gut reactions', and 'my scribble'. This is not the kind of language typically found in formal ceremonies such as prize givings or court examinations. Nor is it the kind of language that you would find in a market research questionnaire. It is idiomatic, meta-phorical and drawing on slang terms. This kind of language displays informality as a contrast to the formality that might be found in those other settings.

Turns are basic units of talk. Interaction is organized around turns. This seems like a rather banal observation – but it is actually pretty important for understanding interaction. Turns can be as little as one word long ('what?'), they can be a phrase ('in the office'), a clause ('when we finish writing this book'), a full sentence ('Joan is going out tonight'), or combinations of these things. These different things are known in conversation analysis as 'turn-construction units'. The boundaries of turn-construction units are places where speaker change becomes relevant.

Turns are very flexible things – which is well and good given the practical role of talk and the immensely varied things it is used to do. The aim of analysis is not to give a definition of what is a well-formed turn; it is very different from grammatical analysis. Rather, the focus is on how turns are treated as complete by participants. Where do they treat speaker change over as appropriate? Where does starting to speak become treated as an interruption?

Sacks, Schegloff and Jefferson (1974) have sketched out some of the basic rules of interaction. These rules do not govern what people say – although interaction tends to follow the rules. Rather they are a normative system that makes departures and deviations notable. Thus when a speaker starts to speak in the midst of another speaker's turn this is a notable thing. It might be treated as rude, or perhaps taken as a sign of intimacy (Coates, 1995, has shown that there is more overlap in talk between people in close relationships).

The turn organization of market research focus groups is an interesting topic in its own right. As we note at various points, speaker change over is often carefully managed by the moderator. And, although the interaction often feels free and fluid, it overwhelmingly centres on the moderator – only rarely do more than one or two exchanges take place between two participants.

Want to know more?

Hutchby and Wooffitt (1998: 47–57) is a good introductory overview. For more depth the original Sacks, Schegloff and Jefferson (1974) paper is hard to beat.

6 DISPLAYING INFORMALITY THROUGH INTONATION

When conversation analysts such as Gail Jefferson were developing systems for transcribing speech into written form one of the features they found they needed to represent was talk said in a humorous or light way. In the absence of an obvious ready-made term for such a way of talking, researchers dubbed it 'smiley voice', which captures the voice quality very effectively. It is talk that sounds like the speaker is smiling. Actual laughter is transcribed as it sounds as far as possible.

We have highlighted a number of moments of smiley voice in our example introduction. As well as any broad contrast that such intonation makes against formal, impersonal ceremonies, this smiley intonation is carefully finessed in with the action. For example, the first smiley intonation comes after the moderator comments on the non-arrival of some of the participants. This is just the kind of activity that might reveal the moderator's irritation or dramatize the trouble ill disciplined group members might get into. By delivering his next utterance with a smiley voice the moderator shows he is not irritated (whether he actually is or not!) and that participant breaches can be taken lightly (although they will be noticed!).

7 MANAGING INFORMALITY THROUGH THE PHYSICAL SETTING

When we looked at the videotapes of many different market research focus groups one thing was immediately apparent. There was a striking uniformity of physical setting. The groups were run in living room sized spaces, with neutral decoration (a symphony of magnolia!) and sometimes one or two tasteful but anonymous pictures on the walls. The one-way mirror typically had opened curtains, giving it something of the effect of a window. For the most part, participants were seated on soft, low furnishings – sofas and chairs – on three sides of a coffee table. The moderator sat on a similar chair on the fourth side of the table, with his or her back to the video. Participants were provided with food and drink – tea, water, coffee and biscuits or cakes.

The exceptions to this are where the size of products becomes an issue. Thus cars and vans, understandably, require a large space and participants need to be able to move among them. In contrast, where the concern is with features of small products the participants may be sat up around a central table giving everyone a clear view.

Again these details may seem trivial and unexceptional. However, they contribute to countering expectations about formality. They suggest a family home rather than a formal office setting or public space. In particular, the participants are not seated behind desks such as in job interviews or in court, or on a raised dais such as with prize giving. Eating and drinking, of course, are things that go on during conversation at home, while in formal ceremonies the eating and drinking are rarely done during the ceremony itself. You open the champagne after the wedding. The more the interaction can suggest a casual conversation over tea, the less the participants are likely to fill their talk with the hedges and qualifications characteristic when the accountability of views is paramount. Tea and biscuits not only keeps the members feeling happy, but works against account clutter.

Summary: facets of informality

There is no recipe for producing informality. It is a complex feature of interaction with a number of different facets to it. We suggest moderators can build informality by combining a number of different facets of talk.

Most directly they can formulate what the interaction is and what it is not in a way that stresses its informality. These explicit formulations can be complemented by constructing the psychological phenomena of interest to be feelings or gut reactions; that is, entities on which the person ought to be able to provide an immediate and spontaneous report, rather than having to carefully weigh up issues or calculate positions. This moderator talk is delivered in a manner that suggests that it is casually ad libbed rather than scripted, using idioms and metaphors that suggest informal interaction, and using a range of light or smiley intonation (which says: this is not a sermon or acceptance speech). All this takes place in a setting that is more like a living room than a standard office over serve-yourself tea and biscuits.

It seems effortless, but there is a lot of moderator work to be done here. They have to work against the idea that they will demand high standards of performance, and that they will be an aloof overseer directing the action from above. The performance is presented as easy, and, indeed, natural; and the moderator is engaged in the process rather than standing aloof like a news interviewer or teacher.

Informality in practice

Up to now we have identified a number of facets to the production of informality and started to consider the way these might be related to achieving the focus group task. We will now move on to illustrate these facets operating together in some examples.

First reactions

The following extract is the introduction to a specific task some time into the group. The participants are being asked for their *first reactions* to advertising ideas.

```
M: Caz      °Right,° (0.6) let me:, (0.4) the time has      some quiet
            come. (0.6)                                     laughter
            *Em if I can find the right boards. (0.2)       Caz searches
            To show you some:, (0.4) advertising            behind sofa
            ideas:. (0.2)*
            No I can't find the right boards.° (0.2)
            °Yes, yes I can° (0.6)
            okay, as you can see we've (h)got (h)a
            (h) <who:le volume> to show you. (0.4)
            U::m, (0.6) °and we'll just sort of° work,
            (0.2) work through these,
            so:, (0.4) the thing I should I should
```

```
        explain before I actually show them
        they're calling these advertising ide:as.
        and, (0.2) look °swanky and so on.° (.)
        Is everyone sort of (.) .hhh °feel about
        that°
        SO:! (0.4) first reactions! (.)
        just (0.2) off >the top of< your head
        Now, .hh (.) e:m, (0.2) .hh the way
        ⌐they've been put together is, (.) they've
        just sort of taken- (0.2) sort of
        literally to:rn images out of magazi:nes
        and things. (.) .hh
        U:m, (.) .hh so they're by no means
        finished y'know.
        We're so: used to seeing in magazines
        particularly like, (.) beautifully crafted
        images aren't we.
        And y'know every single little detail has
        been made to look absolutely wonderful.
        Now, (.) .hhh these are, (.) >y'know<
        thrown together.
        So, .hhh (.) what you've got to do I'm
        afraid, (.) is kind of, (0.2) >see them<
        as cartoons almost.
        But ima:gine them .hhh as they would be      continues
        finished in your, (.) favourite magazine     reading the ad
```

Let us highlight some features of how the moderator introduces this exercise. It probably seems a bit clumsy on a first read through. Yet the surface clumsiness disguises the beautiful way the moderator builds informality. Note the early comments on the search for display boards that are a sotto voce commentary on her actions while she delves behind the sofa. This displays a relaxed and even playful spontaneity. This is not something carefully planned and rehearsed. This combines together with the pattern of pauses and hesitations, and the use of idioms and slang terms ('thrown together', 'swanky'), to show the moderator making up her actions as she goes along.

This spontaneity is picked up in the way the task is presented to the participants. She asks for:

```
first reactions! (.) just (0.2) off >the top of< your head.
```

Providing first *reactions* does not require deep thoughts. Asking for first reactions implies that everybody can cooperate: after all, everyone has first reactions. To ask for correct, concise or original answers would imply a task dependent on ability; asking for first reactions includes everyone. The metaphor the moderator uses – 'off the top of *your head*' – suggests that no mental or physical effort will be necessary. These reactions will be automatically *just there* – sitting on top of your skull, waiting to be picked! Just like the gut feelings participants should provide in our earlier extract they are 'just there' regardless of the kind of person you are: clever or less clever, quick or slow. These are entities on the basis of which no inference should be drawn about the intelligence or the personality of the respondent. This makes them ideal for heading off the worries about accountability.

Easy responses

For most market research questions good moderation will present the participants' task as requiring neither deep nor lengthy thought. It is not a situation where long and careful deliberation is required. The informal and relaxed atmosphere is part of establishing the appropriateness of this spontaneity rather than a deliberative caution. Moderators augment their requests for easy and quick answers with gestures such as snapping their fingers, rolling their hands and waving their arms. Take this example:

```
David        Practical.
M: Carol     Practical, what else.
             (1.0)                                   snaps her
             What would your ideal look like.        finger
             (1.0)
             °say about you (0.2) and your company°
```

Or this one, where the moderator makes a waving hand movement, seemingly in order to encourage contributions:

```
M: Lucy      What else, what=what kind of feelings=
             ((some talk omitted))
             Other? (0.2) Just,                       waves hand
```

Imagine a pair of chess players concentrating on their game, and picture a referee standing next to them gesturing and snapping fingers! This image is bizarre because we think of chess as an activity requiring silence and absorbed attention. Moderators are suggesting something very different from this when they treat these questions as ones that can be answered without thinking or calculation.

Our general point in this section is that the informal style of interaction developed is bound up with the way the research task is presented. It is not something formal and carefully rule bound; it is natural and spontaneous. The implicit message is that the research requires only *easy* answers, produced without any deep thoughts, and *quick* answers which can be delivered in rapid succession. Indeed, more deliberation may produce problems by making people censure what they say, or transform it to what they think the researcher wants.

Combating aloofness

One of the issues in moderation is how to stay neutral. The whole business of the focus group rests on the assumed value of spontaneous expressions of *opinion*. If those opinions appear to have been planted by the moderator, either directly or through some implicit influence, then their validity is called into question. In the next chapter we will consider some of the ways in which moderators achieve neutrality; that is, how they ask questions without planting opinions and how they receive answers without assessing them. However, the requirements of informality pull in the other direction. Informal interaction is not disinterested and aloof; it is partisan and friendly. How is this achieved?

Of course, moderators do not say 'Look, we are friends, and because we are friends you can be as relaxed as possible'. Nevertheless, some of the ways they talk are more characteristic of how friends talk to one another than people in more formal relationships. To put it another way, they work against expectations of neutrality and aloofness. We will pick out two features of this talk, the moderator's use of laughter and their deployment of 'oh'.

Consider the following fragment. It is from a focus group involving shampoo and it involves a participant (Carol) who confesses that she has mixed up hair roots with the television series *Roots*.

```
Carol      when you said roots there and then- (0.2)
           >it was the first< time I thought
           [mm Roots (.) mm the African music          laughing
Sue        [mmm
Carol      y(h)ou kno(h)w (.) but (0.2) >it was< the
           music was overpo:wering [and when you=
Anne                               [mm (.) m
Carol      said [roots (.) its sort of:
Jill            [yeah
           (0.4)
Kate       I lik[ed the music
Carol           [(that's) the tenuous,
           (0.2) very tenu[ous
```

```
→    M: Eve                           [oh Roots as in the T[V
            series
     Carol                                              [yeah
            (.) yeah
→    M: Eve      Heh heh heh heh (and) the book (.)
            [and the-
     Anne       [the-the
     Amy        Music [was (very) strong I felt
     Carol           [well no- not specifically that but
            the- (.) this whole business of
            or(h)ig(h)ins of ma(h)[n (0.2) back to the
            roots (.) an',
```

We will highlight two things the moderator does here which illustrate
ways of resisting aloofness. First, note her use of 'oh' that marks her
realization that the roots in question are associated with television rather
than hair and, second, the subsequent laughter.

Oh and neutrality

The word 'oh' is used in conversation in a number of different ways
(Heritage, 1984b). One of the most central is to mark the receipt of
knowledge or, as John Heritage puts it, a change of knowledge state. This
term is widely used in everyday talk, but it is interestingly rare in
institutional interaction. For example, in television news interviews
although the interviewee is often providing new knowledge in response to
questions it is extremely unusual for the interviewer to use a news receipt
such as oh (just watch an interview on television news – it is easy to
confirm this). This is a standard feature of the institutional organization of
news interviews. The interviewer is not meant to be the recipient of the
news, and certainly not meant to have their own relevant knowledge and
opinions, rather they are meant to facilitate the delivery of news to the
watching audience. In terms of the interaction their role is to be a neutral
conduit. Their stance is 'neutralist' – they display neutrality in their
actions, although this does not mean that they are actually neutral on any
topic.

It is also rare for moderators to receive group member's judgements or
opinions with 'oh' receipts. To do so would probably highlight issues of
their own knowledge or stance on the product. This is something that
could raise questions about neutrality and be potentially consequential for
how participants respond to questions. However, this neutralist stance
risks aloofness. One way of combating this aloofness is to use 'oh' receipts
where they do not disrupt the neutralist stance with respect to opinions on
products. In this case, the moderator 'oh' receipts Karen's acknowledgement of her Roots/roots confusion. In doing this the moderator neatly

In everyday talk people use the particle *oh* to indicate that the story, joke, piece of news or whatever they have been told is new to them. As John Heritage (1984b) puts it, the recipient's knowledge state has been changed; he or she has moved from uninformed to informed. He suggests that there is a general preference in conversation for telling people new information and not telling people things they already know (note the importance of 'as I was just telling these folks' when you are recycling some news for a person who has just arrived). Telling people something they already know is not appreciated.

There are all kind of delicate uses of such a change of state token, but the simplest is where a speaker is validating the newsworthiness of something they are being told about.

```
        Speaker R   I fergot t'tell y'the two best things that
                    happen'tuh me t'day.
 →      Speaker C   Oh super.=What were they
                    (Heritage, 1984b: 303)
```

In everyday conversation ohs are most common in situations where there are questions and answers. Interestingly, work environments where questions and answers are common are marked by the *absence* of ohs. Heritage (1985) considers why this is so in the case of news interviews and courtrooms. In this situation not only are ohs absent, but so are markers of news ('did she?') and assessments ('that's excellent'). He suggests two reasons. First, news receipts such as oh display a commitment to the adequacy of the talk that they receipt. Such a commitment goes against the neutral stance valued in news interviews and courtrooms. Second, talk in news interviews and courtrooms is produced for overhearers – the jury or the news audience. The news receipt token would be inappropriate in such environments as they would suggest that the questioner is the primary addressee of the talk rather than being merely a conduit to jury or audience. By avoiding oh the questioner avoids being the recipient of the report, while maintaining the position of its elicitor.

This is relevant to focus groups where the moderator is maintaining a stance of neutrality with respect to the product and of eliciting talk from the participants for the company or organization that commissioned the group.

Want to know more?

Heritage's (1984b) classic paper on oh is still in the central place. Work on news interviews is summarized in an excellent book by Clayman and Heritage (2002).

shows herself to have understood the source of the confusion and also to be a direct recipient of this knowledge. She has departed from the potentially aloof neutralist stance, but precisely at a point where it is not consequential for knowledge and opinions about the shampoo that is the topic of the group.

Laughter and aloofness

Laughter is a complicated action. Although we tend to think it is some kind of natural reflex that is triggered by a joke or something funny, studies by conversation analysts emphasize that laughter is both used in a wide range of ways and is very finely integrated with interaction (Jefferson et al., 1987).

Laughing at participants is certainly not recommended in standard focus group manuals, which stress that the moderator should be non-judgemental and display warmth and empathy. The moderator's laugh in the above extract is, however, *friendly* in the sense that friends have a good laugh when one of them misunderstands something. Friends are free to laugh at each other. The moderator's laughter mimics this relationship. In laughing at the participant's remark she displays her understanding of the focus group situation as one that allows people to laugh at each other (Glenn, 1995). And this signals that the focus group situation is more akin to the talk that goes on between friends than to the talk that might be expected between professionals and lay people. The moderator here shows herself as an individual, rather than a disinterested expert or someone filling a role.

Our general point is that in using conversational practices like 'oh' receipts and laughter the moderator can work against the aloofness and neutralism of the research situation. However, the skill is in using these practices when they do not cause problems for the moderator's neutrality with respect to participants' knowledge and opinions. We will see in later chapters that it is particularly important for moderators not to become participants who have their own knowledge and opinions about products and services. In this case, confusion over the name of a shampoo presents an opportunity for building the informal nature of the situation and countering its official formal character.

SUMMARY

Part of the art of effective focus group moderation is to generate a situation that is relaxed and informal while still being able to closely manage the interaction. In this chapter we have overviewed some techniques that moderators use to achieve informality.

At the most general, they typically start groups by formulating what the group is and is not. On the one hand, it is characterized as talking or chatting. On the other, it is characterized as not a school classroom or test.

Part of the informality comes from the construction of psychology. The focus is treated as 'gut feelings' or 'top of the head reactions', objects which can be delivered immediately and unthinkingly, and need little or no justification.

The moderator's delivery is an important part of generating informality. In particular, it should work against appearing to be something that is rehearsed or scripted or mechanical. We noted a number of elements to this, including patterns of pauses and hesitancy that suggests moderator talk is being improvised, idiomatic word choice suggestive of informal conversation, and intonation patterns that counter formal or solemn institutional interaction.

These interactional features are complemented by a physical setting suggestive of a living room rather than an office.

Finally, moderators can use various techniques for combating aloofness and neutralism. We noted the way they may have opportunities for using 'oh' receipts and laughing to generate a friendly atmosphere while not compromising the research neutrality with respect to opinions on products. These do no exhaust the techniques for combating aloofness, but are indicative.

TURNING PRACTICES INTO STRATEGIES

STRATEGY ONE
Use the introduction to work against any expectations that the group will be formal and acting as a test of the participants' competence. It is the first place to do this and will 'set the tone' for what comes after.

STRATEGY TWO
Deliver what you are saying in a way that presents it as improvised rather than scripted. Use idiomatic and slang terms that counter expectations of formality and stiffness.

STRATEGY THREE
Be willing to use 'oh' receipts, laughter and other contributions that show you joining in as a person rather than following a role. This will also show that you are being attentive to the group. However, be careful not to use them in a way that makes you become just another participant. That is, do not use them for specific product information, as this will make you appear to be an interested expert in the product.

STRATEGY FOUR
Beware of over-preparation and over-scripting. Take advantage of the spontaneity that comes from working with brief notes or just a checklist of questions. (Strategy two is so important that is worth having it again in different words).

3 Producing Participation

One of the reasons why researchers have turned away from questionnaires and increasingly started to use focus groups is a strong sense that questionnaires constrain people's responses while focus groups allow people to give their views in their own ways and in their own words. One way of looking at this is as an issue of free will and determinism. The questionnaire is a determinist situation where the great risk is that the researcher will merely get back what they put in. The person filling it in is fenced in by limited options and predetermined categories. The more the research participants' actions are determined the more the research risks just chasing its own tail around pre-existing ideas and expectations.

The focus group is a situation of freedom, at least relatively speaking. A whole gang of people are there to speak without a tick box in sight. They can give their own views in their own way and in their own words. However, this freedom is also a *problem* for the moderator. For it lacks precisely what to many is attractive about questionnaires: *control*. In a questionnaire people cannot go 'off message', or tell you about their holiday, feel shy, or start to argue with one another about the biscuits because their only communicative possibility is a tick box. In focus groups the moderator needs to be able to make people speak up, or keep people quiet; they must stop them using their freedom to say too little or too much. It is the very freedom of the group members that generates work for the moderator.

The tool for this moderator work is conversation. As analysts such as Schegloff, Sacks and Heritage (Heritage, 1984a; Sacks, 1992; Schegloff, 1995) have shown, conversation itself is a wonderful mix of freedom and determinism. At any point in talk there is a very wide range of things that can be said, in a very wide variety of different ways, contributed by different participants. And yet rather than a recipe for chaos, conversation is very orderly. Indeed, conversational structures are very robust and open to people with different backgrounds, levels of attentiveness, concerns and so on. We have already noted the way conversation tends to be organized around structures such as adjacency pairs: question and answer, say, or invitation and acceptance. Although uttering the first part of an adjacency pair does not determine what comes next, it does set up a situation where what comes next cannot fail to be related to it.

For example, think of an invitation. If you are invited to dinner and ignore the invitation, the invitation does not thereby disappear or become irrelevant. Instead you become someone who has ignored the invitation, and therefore someone who is rude, or maybe dislikes the speaker. What you say immediately after an invitation has been said in that particular context and is likely to be interpreted in relation to that particular context. That does not mean that uttering an invitation *determines* what comes after. People can accept, reject, manage, put off or otherwise rework invitations in a host of creative ways. Yet they are *orienting* to that invitation.

This adjacency pair organization is there to be exploited by the moderator. They can use an adjacency pair that is familiar to all of us as the basis for a lot of the business of the group. That is the question-answer pair. This pair is particularly useful in that it is asymmetric – asking questions is a very different thing from answering them and, obviously, answering questions is a way of conveying information. So, that's sorted then, on to the next chapter? Well, no, it is more complicated than that! Asking questions turns out to be a rather tricky thing to do. Questions turn out to be rather more complex things than school grammar books suggest.

The dilemma of asking

When we think about questions it is useful to distinguish what can loosely be called *real* questions from *exam* questions. With real questions the speaker actually wants to know the answer because they do not know what the answer is. In contrast, with exam questions the questioner already knows the answer, and is checking whether the person who has been asked the question knows that answer.

The first thing to note about focus groups is that moderators are keen that their questions are not heard as exam questions. This can be done in three ways. The first is rather explicit. Moderators regularly say 'it's not like in school or anything like that'. We saw an example of this in the previous chapter. Second, they can stress the informal nature of what is going on. If we are taking part in a chat we are not being tested: 'I think we will have a chat today about shampoo'. Third, moderators can present themselves as in the same position as group members with respect to the object being examined. Here is an example from a moderator we have called Saul:

```
M: Saul      Em, (0.8) let me just tell you who ↑I am
             so that you're clear.
             Em (1.2) I work for a (0.2) a little known
             company called Zappy Research, but we're
             an independent market research company.
```

```
(0.4) And that independent bit is (.) the
most important thing about us.
Because, (0.4) you'll see tonight (0.4)
>that we're looking at< some advertising
i↑deas, (0.6) e:m, (0.4) we:, (0.4)
>didn't have anything< to do with these
ideas, (0.2) we didn't cre↑ate them, (0.6)
I'm not gonna get upset if you hate them
and I don't get a bonus if you love em
```

                                    continues

By stressing that his company did not create the ideas, Saul is showing that he will not be offended by criticism. Not only does this discourage group members from thinking they ought to be positive, it also suggests that with respect to the adverts they have the same status. They are all looking at somebody else's ideas.

It is tempting to think of this just in terms of generating a relaxed atmosphere and discouraging people from being guarded about negative opinions. However, there is a more direct and practical issue. If the asymmetry between questioner and answerer is too strong, if the questions seem too much like exam questions, it will make what is going on seem like a test where there is a right or wrong answer. It is not just that this will inhibit the participation that is crucial for a smoothly running group; it is that people will be highly focused on the *accountability* of the answers. The more people are concerned with the possible *inadequacy* of what they are saying the more they will preface their answers with 'it seems to me', 'I am not sure, but', and follow their answers with justifications and elaborate appeals to evidence. What we will find is answers that are full of what we have called *account clutter*. Accountability is a pervasive concern, so it will not be possible or desirable to eliminate it fully – that way chaos lies! But it can be minimized by asking questions in the right way. This will avoid as much of the clutter as possible. Also, as we will see later, some accounts are crucial for market research.

So how can questions be asked to eliminate this account clutter? To help understand this we will need to consider a bit more how information is elicited in everyday situations, as well as other institutional situations.

Indirect information eliciting

Questions are powerful because when they are asked an answer becomes due. Not answering is both noticeable and accountable; questioners monitor closely for answers and non-answerers typically account for their non-answer. This is easily seen in studies of interaction where when an answer is not delivered it continues to be treated as relevant or pending – Schegloff

---

Conversation Box 3.1
The importance of display

Visibility is central to interaction and people's accountability in interaction. Talk is a public medium where doing an action and being seen to be doing an action work hand in hand. Speakers show that they have made an invitation; recipients show that they have understood it as in invitation, and maybe show pleasure about being invited. Such display can be phoney or incompetent on occasion, but interaction would not work without it.

The centrality of display is reflected in our language for writing about focus group interaction. We write about a 'display of informality' or a ·participant 'displaying her opinion' as this highlights the social, interactional nature of these things.

Want to know more?

In his classic lectures on conversation Sacks (1992) repeatedly considers the issue of observation and observability in interaction. Try, for example, Lecture 13, 'Button-button who's got the button'.

(1968) calls this *conditional relevance*. And when people don't answer they typically give reasons: 'I don't know', 'I'd like to tell you but I told Brian I wouldn't', 'I'll be in a better position to answer that after 3 o'clock'. This power is not something to be used lightly, though. It makes questioning potentially invasive. Questions can 'put people on the spot'. As we have seen, conversationalists are very sensitive to the concerns of recipients. Think of the careful way in which Lesley extended that invitation to Arnold that we discussed in Chapter 1 – she avoids putting him on the spot.

In everyday situations people often avoid asking direct questions, rather they indirectly elicit information through fishing. Anita Pomerantz (1980) has shown the way that fishing works. The basic form is to say something about your side of a situation that your addressee may know more about. This gives them the opportunity to fill in their side. So one of us gets a knock on the door, and Mick enters: 'Oh Mick, you're at work'. On the face of it, this seems a pretty odd thing to say as Mick clearly knows he is at work! Yet, in the context of him having said the day before that he wasn't coming in it provides an opportunity for him to explain: 'I realized I had to go to the staff meeting'. Note that this indirect way of asking is less invasive or challenging. 'Why are you in, you said you weren't coming in' sounds very much like a challenge. Fishing by providing your side of the situation creates an environment for giving the relevant information (or withholding it) with less of the pressure that comes from dealing with a question.

Although fishing like this is common in everyday situations, and in some institutional situations such as therapy (Peräkylä, 1995), it is very rare in focus groups. This might be because the opportunities to give a relevant 'side' are less common, or because of the problem in singling out a particular individual; it might put them on the spot as much as a direct question. Here is an example that shows what fishing might look like and why it might not appear very often.

```
   M: Yvonne    What ↑words would you use to describe this
                van.
                (0.8)
   David        Su↑perb                                    some
                (2.0)                                      participants
   M: Yvonne    ↑Yeah (0.4) what else                      laugh
   David        Sporty. (0.2) trendy.
                (1.0)
→  M: Yvonne    What about the rest of you you're pulling
                faces. You're going. (0.2) you're shaking
                your head. (1.0)
                Tell me what words you'd use to describe    some soft
                this van                                    laughter
   Alan         °can you can you say this van is like
                sporty and trendy°
```

Note the way moderator Yvonne fishes. She does not *directly* ask about their face pulling or head shaking, or about the inferred disagreement. Rather she describes what she can *see*. In the arrowed turn we see her addressing the group: 'you're pulling faces' and then homing in on an individual member 'you're shaking your head'. Whether it is a problem with singling out, or putting on the spot, the fishing does not get a response. Indeed, after a pause of a second she moves back to asking Alan a direct question.

This may seem like a bit of a detour. However, we have wanted to show the importance of two points. First, asking questions can be a tricky business. It can be invasive and it can highlight asymmetries between questioner and answerer. Second, it shows that the sort of fishing seen in everyday settings is difficult to manage effectively in focus groups, so rather rare.

In the rest of the chapter we describe the two information elicitation techniques that are most common in focus groups. They are:

- elaborate questions;
- minimal questions.

We will consider them in turn.

Asking elaborate questions

If there is one thing that most of the existing manuals tend to agree on it is that the questions moderators ask should be simple, unambiguous and unelaborated. They often provide made up examples to highlight precisely this feature. Interestingly, however, when we look at *actual* questions in *actual* focus groups many of them are far from simple (Puchta and Potter, 1999). And, moreover, the way questions are asked in focus groups is highly regular. Specifically, the questions asked at the start of particular topics or themes are almost always quite elaborate with a number of different components to them, while the follow up questions within a topic or theme are almost always quite simple.

Let us start by considering elaborate questions that play a major role at the start of topics. In our discussion above we noted that asking questions can be a tricky business. We suggest that in focus groups the elaboration is there to manage this trickiness. In particular, it is there to:

- display informality,
- guide participants without forcing them,
- secure participation,
- manage asymmetry between moderator and participant.

The best way to show how this works is with an example. This is a group taking place in a large hall where a number of different cars are being discussed. As they walk from car to car two camera operators follow them to capture the action.

```
1→   M: Walt    Is your image of these two vehicles:
                diff'rent. (1.4) You look at the [Car A]
                (.) you look at the [Car B] you feel >that
                they're< the same ↑kind of vehicle? (0.2)
                .hhh You see them being used in the same
                ↑way: by the same peo:ple? Or >do you< is
                [there a slight differ↓ence.]
     Bruce      [       °No (.) no°        ]
                (0.6)
     Alan       °no (0.2) not (  )°
     Tim        >In some way but I see them< (.) 'spect
                that's a younger ↑image::, (.) somehow.
     Stewart    °possibly yeah°
                (0.4)
2→   M: Walt    Possibly younger im[age,
     Tim                           [yeah,
     M: Walt    Why do you say (that)
     Tim        >Just the< ↑overall sty:le, (0.4) design.
                ((continues))
```

The most obvious thing about this extract is the contrast between Walt's first question (at arrow 1), which has a complex structure with a number of different components and the simple questions he asks later (arrow 2). Let us focus on Walt's first question. It starts with something that looks rather like a simple question:

```
Is your image of these two vehicles different.
```

The group members do not answer at this point. They wait; and moderator Walt unpacks the question, specifying what it means and what it refers to, rather more precisely. He suggests the members look at the two cars and see if they 'feel they are the same kind of vehicle'.

This unpacking and specifying is a common feature of elaborate questions at the start of topics. They are needed because focus groups are an unfamiliar situation to the participants. The vast majority of group members are taking part for the first time. And however explicit seeming, questions typically offer a very wide range of possible ways of answering them. People prefer not to answer than to answer and then need to be corrected for giving a response that misses the point. Unpacking helps *secure participation*.

Moderator Walt does not only specify the meaning of the question further, he also goes on to provide candidate answers. Such as 'You see them being used in the same way by the same people' and 'there is a slight difference'. This provides a further guide to what is appropriate. Appropriate answers should look like these answers. That is, the candidate answers provide a *guide* for the participants.

In addition, providing an array of candidate responses makes it harder for members to give silent or 'don't know' responses. At minimum, participants ought to be able to select one or other option. The candidate response array is a further way of helping *secure participation*.

Now let's pick out another feature of Walt's elaborate question. He asks about the *image* the participants have of the cars, about what they *feel*, and the differences they *see*. These little words may look rather unimportant, but they are fundamental for managing the asymmetry between researcher and researched. The questions ask about the participants' own perspective. That is, they ask about something that the participants not only know about, but know about in a privileged way; they are the only people who properly know about it. Put another way, these are real questions, not exam questions where there is a predetermined right answer. If the moderator had asked about the *actual* differences between the two cars he would have generated an exam situation where group members could be corrected for making mistakes. These issues will come to the fore in the next chapter.

Take the following elaborate question to illustrate the way moderators stress this. Moderator Karen is asking a relatively straightforward question that builds and extends a theme that has already been introduced about baby products.

```
M: Karen    Apart from, (.) apart from this >kind of<
            baby product, and Mothercare and things
            what other, (0.2) what other areas, (0.6)
            use: imagery like that. (0.2) >I mean<
            °what else have you seen°=
Bea         =Vitamin tablets
```

What is interesting here is the way that Karen elaborates the question. She changes it from 'what other areas of baby product use imagery like that' to 'what else have you seen'. That is, she changes from a question that is potentially a factual one, with a right or wrong answer that the moderator might know, to a subjective one that only the participants are able to answer about him or herself. Indeed, once rephrased one of the participants answers instantly.

Again, asking the question in this way helps *secure participation*. Not only does the question generate an environment where there is no right or wrong answer, it also constructs the answer as the kind of thing that anyone ought to know about himself or herself.

Finally, let us note another feature of moderator Walt's elaborate question. The way the question is developed displays it as made up, as unfolded in the course of the interaction. Walt is not reading from a sheet and his question does not *sound* memorized (although one of the skills of oratory is to memorize things to make them sound fabricated on the spot). He scans the group as he speaks, and his elaboration is at least partly tuned to their hesitancy.

This has two important consequences. First it *displays informality*; it is not following a set script or formal procedure. This encourages participants to contribute in a relaxed way, without spending a lot of time managing the accountability of what they say. That is, it *discourages account clutter*. Second, it *displays attentiveness* to the group, which not only encourages them to view their contributions as valued, but indicates that they are being closely monitored. It thus encourages people to *stay focused*.

We can give a schematic outline of the typical pattern of elaborate questions.

Moderator   Asks question
            Reinterates question
            Offers candidate answer 1

Offers candidate answer 2
Reiterates question

There is a range of ways in which questions can be elaborated. More reiterations can be provided, or more candidate answers. If we return to Walt's elaborated question in the above extract we can review its features.

```
M: Walt   Is your image of these two vehicles:      asks question
          ↓diff'rent.
          (1.4)
          You look at the [Car A] (.) you look      reiterates question
          at the [Car B] you feel >that they're<
          the same ↑kind of vehicle?
          (0.2) .hhh
          You see them being used in the same       candidate answer 1
          ↑way: by the same peo:ple?
          Or >do you< is there a slight             candidate answer 2
          differ↓ence.
```

The general picture we are wishing to paint here is of questions being built in a complex manner to deal with a number of potential difficulties simultaneously. Asking such questions in the way described here is undoubtedly one of the key skills involved in running successful focus groups. The kind of guidance they offer is one of the things that distinguishes answering focus group questions from answering questions in written questionnaires. It is therefore somewhat ironic that writing about focus groups has often advised moderators to ask questions as if they came straight from a written questionnaire.

Minimal questions

As we said above, elaborate questions tend to be used when new topics or question types are introduced. They are common in focus groups. However, minimal questions are also common. They tend to be used where:

- an individual member is asked a follow-up question;
- a *specific* answer is required from the group.

We will start with the latter class of questions, as they are less interesting.

Conversation analysis and discursive psychology are both approaches that are concerned with actions and interaction as public and social phenomena. They are not trying to explain how people talk by reference to underlying mental states such as attitudes or strategies. Indeed, discursive psychology is specifically interested in how these things are constructed in and for interaction. How does someone construct an 'attitude' when agreeing with a prior speaker? How does a person use the notion of strategy to make their actions seem sensible and accountable?

These approaches are left with a problem when writing about interaction. The language we use for describing interaction tends to default to ideas of strategy and intention. We need some way of talking and writing about people doing things actively without making unhelpful cognitive assumptions about that. The idea of orienting provides one solution. Plants can actively orient to the light, but few of us think that they are intending or planning to do that!

Take this example. When speakers make lists to describe and summarize things (not when they are going shopping) they are regularly made up of three items. Jefferson has shown that listeners orient to this three-part feature by being less likely to interrupt before a possible third part. Speakers orient to it by often adding a 'generalized list completer' if they do not have a third easily available.

```
        Heather:   And they had like a concession stand like at
                   a fair where you can buy
1   →              Coke
2   →              and popcorn
3   →              and that type of thing.
                   (from Jefferson, 1990: 66)
```

This speaker is orienting to the requirement for a proper list having three parts.

Want to know more?

Try Potter (1998b) on the way cognition is understood in the analysis of interaction.

Minimal questions with specific answers

Focus groups are complex situations where the moderator has to manage a group of half a dozen or more people for a considerable length of time. All kinds of business has to be sorted out; some closely related to the research task, some more generally related to the smooth running of the interaction. These tasks can involve simple minimal questions. For example, in this group a task has involved placing magnetic counters on a scale from light to strong. Moderator Bella in the following example needs to clarify who put a particular counter on the scale.

```
M: Bella    ↑Um, (.) I'm always of course interested,
            first of all in the <outliers,> (.)
→           <°who pinned that point there?°>         points to
                                                      clipboard
```

Isabella asks this simple question in a situation where there is a single correct answer. This is a hard fact – one or other group member put the counter in this place – and does not have to be managed in any special way. When appropriate, moderator questions can be, and should be, clear and simple. This reminds us that moderators are not just being verbose for the sake of it, question elaboration is done for specific interactional reasons.

The more common minimal questions in groups are follow-up questions to elaborate questions.

Follow-up Questions

Once things have been got going with an elaborate question, and participants start to respond, the moderator can follow up their responses, asking for clarification or further specific actions. In a sense the elaborate question has set up a frame that is a backdrop for the simpler questions that follow. That is, they are dependent on the earlier more elaborate work.

Here is another example from the same car group as before. It illustrates the contrast between the elaborate opening question and the simple follow-up questions, as well as indicating some of the different types of follow up.

```
M: Walt    E::m, (1.0) this type of fabric. (0.2)
           Okay here, (.) these are little vinyl
           swatches. (0.6)
           Notice in most of the vehicles you have
           (0.2) >parts of (the) fabric and then
           there's vinyl accenting throughout.<
           (0.4) .hh U:m, so these are different,
           (0.4) e::h, (0.2) types of things >that<
           could be available. (0.4) You look at
           the:se. (0.2) Look at patterns, (0.2)
           >I mean you look< at the colours, (.)
           e:m, (.) your feeling is what.
           What, (1.2) >what< image would this give
           you of the vehicle.
           (1.2)
```

```
         Peter      °Cheap.°
         David      hm.
                    (1.0)
         Gisa       °They're too loud aren't they.°
         Carl       too loud [and over the top
         Peter               [yeah
         George     You get tired of them very quickly.
                    (1.0)
1→       M: Walt    Okay, (0.4) what kind of vehicle would
                    you put the:se in.
                    (0.6)
         Peter      [ >Slow one< ]                           some soft
         Gisa       [A:          ] you:ng,                    laughter
         Gisa       *immature*                                smiley voice
         Peter      Bumper car
         Jeff       Kids car
2→       M: Walt    Young, immature,
                    (.)
         Gisa       *Italian,*                                smiley voice
                    (0.6)
         Carl       °Surfers°
3→       M: Walt    Surfers. (0.2) What do you mean by that.
                    (.)
         Carl       >Y'know< like a beach bum >y'know sort
                    of< wants to go down the beach early in
                    the morning and, (0.2) pick up a few
                    girls in the >evening=probably
                    wonderful.<
```

Note the way moderator Walt starts the sequence off with an elaborate question. This has the various characteristics we have emphasized so far. It unpacks and further specifies the question; it asks about members' subjective and therefore privileged views; it displays informality as it is developed in an improvised, ad hoc manner.

Now contrast it with Walt's subsequent contributions:

```
1  Okay, (0.4) what kind of vehicle would you put the:se in.
2  Young, immature,
3  Surfers. (0.2) What do you mean by that.
```

Each of these is brief and straightforward. They include neither elaborations nor displays of informality. It seems that once the elaborate question has done its work and the participants are starting to offer their responses the moderator can go into a very different mode of interaction. Once participants are on board the moderator can go on to ask for more detail (e.g. arrow 1 above), or show he has received a response (e.g. arrow 2 above) or show he has received a response and asked for further specification or unpacking (arrow 3 above).

We are going to have quite a lot to say in later chapters about the kind of responses in which the moderator repeats key terms used by the participants. For the moment, we concentrate on the simple questions: 'what kind of vehicle would you put these in' and 'what do you mean by that'.

What we see is that once people have started to respond they can be questioned further in a direct manner. In effect, having gone on the record with some claim then the moderator treats that claim as something that can be explicated or further unpacked. Having secured participation, further modification of responding is less of a challenge. People's talk is treated as accountable, so there is an expectation that they will be able to elaborate on what they have said. The difference between the elaborate and simple question is that the simple question is not trying to elicit something from scratch, but to develop something that has already been elicited.

Such simple follow up questions can be directed at the group as a whole. Take our first example from above.

```
M: Walt      Okay. (0.4) what kind of vehicle would
             you put the:se in.
             (0.6)
Peter        [ >Slow one< ]                        some soft
Gisa         [A:           ] you:ng,               laughter
Gisa         *immature*                            smiley voice
Peter        Bumper car
Jeff         Kids car
```

Here a number of group members have already offered responses to his elaborate question. Walt now asks a question that is mostly a reordered segment of the original. It is not addressed to any particular individual. It is designed to keep the contributions going; it may fill in a possible silence, put further pressure on those that have not yet contributed to speak, and provide participants time to consider answers.

Follow-up questions to the group as a whole are likely to recycle components from the original elaborate question. Follow-up questions to individuals are rather different. They select an individual by their placement (straight after a person's response), often by gaze, gesture and body orientation, by repeating words from the response, and sometimes by direct questioning.

Look again at the sequence where moderator Walt is asking about fabrics. He follows up Carl's rather quiet 'surfing' response with a simple question.

```
M: Walt      Surfers. (0.2) What do you mean by that.
             (.)
Carl         >Y'know< like a beach bum >y'know sort
             of< wants to go down the beach early in
             the morning and, (0.2) pick up a few
             girls in the >evening=probably
             wonderful.<
```

In response to the moderator's direct follow up, Carl paints a rich and effective picture of the sort of associations of the vehicle done out in the colour that is up for consideration. Here the moderator is successful in eliciting further contribution from Carl.

Follow-up questions are often successful – but they are not guaranteed. Group members may simply treat their responses as sufficient without further explication. Or, of course, the interaction can just get into problems through clumsiness or lack of attention. It is not always easy to separate what the source of the problem is. The following sequence is from a group considering different vans. It illustrates a typically elaborate question opening the topic, and then a series of follow-up questions. The thing to note here is the trouble that emerges late in the extract.

```
M: Eve       Em, (1.6) when you were considering
             your van=what >were the< sorts of
             things that you looked at=what were
             <really critical> things that you
             >were< looking ↓fo:r. (0.4) in your
             va:n.
             (1.0)
Paul         Spa[ce=
Kevin           [Space=
M: Eve       =Space. (0.4) .hh Wha- what kind of
             space, =an-.
             (.)
Kevin        Height                                    Moderator
             (2.0)                                      writes word
                                                        on the
                                                        whiteboard
M: Eve       Height (0.4) >yeah,<
                ((about 8 turns omitted))
```

Robbie	And a decent driving position, cos' y'r sat in it for something like six hours		Moderator noisily moves whiteboard closer to the participants
	(0.6)		
Robbie	[(what)]		
→ M: Eve	[Dr]iving position ((said in a questioning voice))		Moderator continues writing on the whiteboard
Robbie	Yeah cos you don't wanna get out like a cripple		
	(1.0)		
→ M: Eve	So tell me what >you< mean by driving posit<u>io</u>n.		Moderator continues writing Robbie turns to smile at another group member
	(0.4)		
Robbie	Pardon?		
→ M: Eve	What d'you mean by <d<u>ri</u>ving> position (0.2) [Explain.]		
Robbie	[The seat] (0.2) the seat. i- i- i- i- it has to be the ri- dri- it has to feel <u>right</u> when you'>re< driving.		

In this sequence we see moderator Eve starts with an elaborate question. She then follows up on the answer 'space' that Paul and Kevin both give and Paul unpacks 'space' as 'height'. Eve shows the appropriateness and usefulness of this response by writing it on a whiteboard. All well and good so far – a perfect exemplification of a smoothly running group.

Now note what happens when Robbie offers another thing that is important with a van: driving position. Robbie goes on to explicate what he means – it is to do with the length of time that van drivers spend in the seat. Yet simultaneously Eve is moving the whiteboard closer to the group with a scraping noise that partially obscures what Robbie is saying. Eve now repeats 'driving position' with a questioning intonation, ignoring the partially obscured explication that has already been provided. Robbie has another go at what he wants from driving position – you don't get out 'like a cripple'. Perhaps Eve is after one-word answers than can be put on the whiteboard or perhaps she misses its significance because she is writing. Whatever, she treats this as inadequate and asks for further explication.

This is real trouble. Robbie has already given two accounts for his driving position claim. If neither of these is sufficient, perhaps he is confused about what is going on. It is not surprising that he is not sure he has heard Eve right when she asks him *again* to 'tell me what you mean by driving position'. When she repeats this question he struggles to produce what is, in the end, a rather bland answer about it 'feeling right'.

This example illustrates two points. First, follow-up questions are not *guaranteed* to be successful in eliciting further contributions. They may get to a point where people cannot unpack any further. Second, follow-up questions are often successful, but whatever goes on in a group the moderator needs to be *attentive* throughout.

Opinion talk and I don't knows

As a final topic for this chapter we will discuss the role of opinion talk in heading off answers such as 'I don't know'. It is common to think about opinions as useful information for market research. That is, they are typically thought about as a *topic* of research. From our perspective opinions have another use that is more to do with what they contribute to the interaction. One thing opinions can be useful for is constructing questions that are answerable (or are hard to resist answering). Opinion questions are not easily answered with the 'it depends' and 'I don't know' responses that drive market researchers to an early grave. Such responses are more characteristic of factual questions, where participants can appropriately claim insufficient knowledge or emphasize their lack of certainty. Focus group moderators stress that opinions are immediate rather than thought out, certain rather than doubtful, and things that are neither right nor wrong. In other words, asking for opinions is an effective way of getting answers out of the participants rather than accounts for why they cannot provide answers.

Let us take a brief example to see this in operation. In the extract that follows we see the moderator emphasizing opinions in the face of an 'it depends' response.

```
     M: Alan    °Is that a good name.°
                (.)                                member clears
                >for this< brand. (.) or?          throat
                (.)
→    Jake       It depends. how it tastes.
                [well. because taste] (like) *the name*    smiley voice
     M: Alan    [Yes. (.) you.      ]
                (1.3)
```

→   You would, (.) well you don't know it
                       °yet.° Just from your, (.) your <u>gut</u>   member coughs
                       feeling.
                       (3.4)
Owen   Well, (.) it hasn't got any message.

When Jake is asked about the quality of the brand name he gives an 'it depends' response. Note how quickly moderator Alan picks up on this. As soon as Jake has said 'it depends how it tastes' moderator Alan cuts in (while Jake continues to speak). When Jake ends and he has the floor moderator Alan does another version of the question, and this asks specifically for 'gut feeling'. This elicits a (rather simplistic) assessment: Well it hasn't got any message. Asking for 'spontaneous impressions' or 'gut feelings' diverts participants' objections and displayed difficulties in answering questions. More generally, asking for opinions and feelings can be a device to counter 'it depends' answers.

SUMMARY

We started this chapter with the big issue of freedom versus determinism. One of the things that attracts researchers to focus groups is the possibility of allowing research participants freedom to address issues in their own way, in their own words. Focus groups represent an oasis of freedom in the big determinist desert of questionnaires. Yet the problem is in managing this freedom; how is what is going on able to be both free and fashioned into a research setting? How can participation be secured yet in a way that is not (overly) constrained?

We suggested that groups exploit basic features of the way conversation is organized into adjacency pairs. Although the first part of the pair does not determine what comes next, it sets up the environment for what comes next. In particular, questions do not determine answers, but they do set up an environment where answers are expected and appropriate.

Things are more complex than this. Asking questions generates an unhelpful dilemma. For it is easy for questions to be heard as exam questions where group members are being tested on the adequacy of their responses. This will be very inhibiting. People may be reluctant to contribute responses that may be identified as mistaken. And when they do contribute responses they may drown them in account clutter.

In everyday situations there is a range of indirect ways of eliciting, including fishing for responses. However, these are rare in focus groups. The predominant form of eliciting participation involves two kinds of questions. The first is *elaborate questions*. These manage the dilemma of asking and encourage participation by including a range of elements.

- *Informality*: They are delivered as if improvised. This displays informality and suggests that the moderator is not following a script that might indicate that right or wrong answers are appropriate.
- *Unpacking*: The question is reworked and rephrased. This clarifies the way the question should be approached (and perhaps indicates that it does not have a single meaning). This helps secure participation.
- *Candidate answers*: Elaborate questions typically provide one or more candidate answers. These help indicate what will be treated as appropriate. Their provision makes it harder for participants to avoid responding.
- *Psychological terms*: Questions focus on feelings, seeing, noticing and so on. This places the group members in a privileged position to answer the questions. It simultaneously counters the members' worry that they may fail to offer the correct answer to an exam question.

Questions like these are quite different from other familiar formal situations. They counter the kind of authority and knowledge differential seen in classrooms, say, or medical consultations. Focus group participants must not feel they are amateurs to the expert moderators; elaborate questions are designed to make them the experts in their own beliefs and feelings.

Once elaborate questions have been used to elicit and guide participants' responding, these can be followed up by *simple questions*. These simple follow-up questions depend on the framing already performed by the elaborate questions.

- They can be addressed to the *group* asking for further alternatives to responses already given.
- Or they can be addressed to a particular *individual*, asking them to unpack a particular response.

Both elaborate and simple questions are crucial to eliciting participation. Each is ideally suitable for a different environment.

TURNING PRACTICES INTO STRATEGIES

STRATEGY ONE
At the start of new topics and themes ask elaborate questions in a way that shows uncertainty both about the answer and the type of answer. Unpack it as it goes along. Include a range of candidate answers. Make the participants experts by focusing on views, opinions or feelings.

STRATEGY TWO
Once elaborate questions have got participants on board then they can be followed up with minimal questions. These can generate more group responses or can get individuals to unpack particular responses.

STRATEGY THREE

Participants' answers can be treated as incomplete *glosses* for what they *really* want to say. This should both generate more explicit or complete answers and further present participants as the experts in their own *universe*.

STRATEGY FOUR

Pay attention to the participants. Watch how attentive they are to you and to each other. Show the participants that you are paying attention to them.

4 Producing Opinions

This chapter centres on the issue of what precisely focus groups produce, and how moderators can help with that production. One of the surprising things about focus groups is the degree of vagueness of what their product is. Focus groups are summarized in brief reports, and the video record is often made available for use. Yet the upshot is rarely made more explicit than this, at least in common social science terms. This is rather different from a questionnaire or opinion poll where there is typically some simple bottom line finding such as that 45 per cent of respondents say they will vote Labour in an election. Focus group summaries often use participants' own words or phrases rather than attempting to transform them into technical social science terms.

Moderators put quite a lot of effort into explaining what focus groups are about when they open groups. Yet their explanations typically reflect this vagueness. Indeed, they often focus much more on what focus groups are *not* about than what they *are* about. We will suggest that this vagueness is not a problem. Rather, it is a practical part of running quality focus groups.

This vagueness is mirrored in the existing books and manuals for focus group moderation. These sometimes describe the aim as being to identify POBAs. This is an acronym coined by the American market researcher Naomi Henderson (1991) to stand for Perceptions, Opinions, Beliefs and Attitudes. POBA combines a range of more or less technical psychological terms such as 'attitude' with more or less everyday psychological terms such as 'perception'. This sounds a bit like a fudge – after all, there are rather important differences between these things and they are often loosely understood in themselves, let alone in combination. And indeed it is a fudge. Yet our suggestion is that it is a rather helpful one.

We do not want moderators and writers about focus groups to sort out the tensions in their ideas and come to a clearer definition. Rather to the contrary, we think that this vagueness is there for at least three good reasons.

First, it is a result of the tension between the social science origins of market research focus groups, which were developed with the technical terminology that was available at that time, and the practicalities of dealing with people producing evaluations in groups. The looseness has stopped this tension becoming a problem. If focus groups were brought into line with some of the more technical social science concepts they would become more clumsy with their approach to interaction.

Second, the vagueness of POBAs reflects the lack of a one-to-one relationship between evaluations and particular words or psychological objects. For example, someone may evaluate a film by saying that they *don't like it* or that it is *not very good*. The former references the speaker's preferences (in social science language their attitudes, perhaps, or their opinions); the latter references characteristics of the world. These evaluations have a different logic.

Third, the looseness of the idea of POBAs allows it to encompass the fluidity of people's everyday evaluative practices, where people may move between evaluations done directly and evaluations done indirectly via positive or negative descriptions. Moreover, there is a whole range of descriptions which may, or may not, be evaluative, but can be a major part of what focus groups produce.

We will need to consider each of these themes if we are going to come to a better understanding of how moderators can generate interesting, er, 'material' (we are going to be cautious about what the product is for the moment). Each of them will be discussed in the course of the chapter.

We will start with a consideration of the traditional social science notions of attitudes that form the backdrop to focus group research. Then we will look at some of the ways that evaluations are done in everyday settings, and the problems that this raises for traditional notions. After that we will look at how the vagueness about the findings of focus groups is reflected in the way moderators introduce groups to the new members. Finally, we will consider some of the detailed ways in which moderators can both *exploit* the logic of evaluation to generate good material and circumvent some of the problems with interaction that evaluations generate.

Attitudes and evaluations

If we were pushed into identifying one particular thing as the product of focus groups the most likely candidate would be attitudes. Focus groups produce attitudes about products, services, politicians, social issues or whatever. The attitude concept is one of the oldest in social psychology. Despite its long history, it is not easy to define precisely. Indeed, definitions often equally rely on problem terms such as 'view', 'feeling', 'preference' or 'judgement'. In a telling observation, Gordon Allport (1935), who was one of the key figures in early social psychology, suggested that its very imprecision is one of the features that has made the notion so popular. It allows tricky theoretical tensions to be glossed over. This prefigures our own observations with respect to focus groups.

Defining attitudes

Let us spend a little time considering the technical notion of attitudes using one of the most respected recent definitions. This will help us in considering some of the things that go on in focus groups. Mark Zanna and John Rempel define attitudes as follows:

> we regard an attitude as the categorization of a stimulus object along an evaluative dimension based upon, or generated from, three general classes of information: (1) cognitive information, (2) affective/emotional information, and/or (3) information concerning past behaviours. (1988: 319)

Lets unpack this a bit. The emphasis on *categorization* recognizes that to evaluate something you need to categorize it. If you think a particular chocolate bar or politician is a good thing then you need to be able to pick out that bar or politician to be able to do the assessment. Social psychologists are often nostalgic for their behaviourist past, hence the description of what is evaluated as a *stimulus object* with its connotations of the 'stimulus-response' psychology of rats in mazes. But it is just a way of talking about the thing that the attitude is about.

The emphasis on *evaluative dimensions* notes that attitudes can evaluate things in various different ways. For example, judgements can be absolute – Snickers bars are very good – or relative – Snickers bars are better than Mars bars. Finally, the definition includes a story about how attitudes are formed – they come from information of three kinds. These kinds are emphasized in a wide range of studies of attitudes that have highlighted ways in which they can be generated or changed.

Cognitive information is simply ideas, beliefs, remembered events, and so on. Did you find that last time you bought this shampoo it was rather sticky? Have you read about chaos and inequality that arises in countries that use private health insurance schemes rather than publicly funded health systems?

Affective/emotional information comes from feelings. You might like that shampoo because it reminds you of a reassuring childhood shampoo. You might simply feel good about a public health system and feel private systems are cold and selfish.

Information concerning past behaviours highlights the importance of how we acted in the past to how we act now. We may buy a Snickers bar simply because that is what we did last time. We went to the state doctor because that is what we always do. Rather paradoxically, this emphasizes that we sometimes work out our preferences indirectly from what we did in the past.

This is a sophisticated definition, and probably one of the best available when considering attitudes. We have indicated some limitations of the idea of attitudes in Chapter 1. The point is not that the definition is flawed, or that the notion of attitudes does not have its uses. It is that the attitude notion was developed without looking carefully at how people *use* evaluations in actual settings, and what they *do* with them. As we noted, even sophisticated discussions of attitudes, such as Zanna and Rempel's, tend to treat attitudes as relatively static internal positions. The person goes through some kind of unconscious mental calculation using information about feelings or past behaviours, and the upshot is a position on a dimension.

It is worth reiterating the limitations of this view:

- It treats attitudes as cognitive objects rather than looking at evaluations done as parts of practices.
- It takes evaluations out of their position in arguments where alternatives are possible.
- It treats the stimulus object as a straightforwardly existing thing that is evaluated, rather than considering the way objects are constructed via evaluations.

Let us explore this a bit further. Our general point will be that focus groups are interactional, conversational encounters. If we are going to understand what is going on in them we will need to go beyond the abstract cognitive notion of attitudes, which tends to be static and individual, and consider the way evaluations are produced and managed when people are in conversation with others.

Beyond attitudes

Let us just remind ourselves where we are in terms of the contrast between traditional and discursive approaches. In traditional attitude theory attitudes are considered to be separate from the 'stimulus object'; they are seen as individual possessions; they are seen as abstract evaluations. In discursive psychology the focus is on interaction, and each of these key features is understood differently. The fundamental shift, of course, is towards looking at evaluations rather than attitudes. More specifically, the shift is to seeing evaluations as developed, in part, through constructing the

---

Conversation Box 4.1
Formulations

One of the features of talk in institutional settings such as school classrooms, police interrogations, or television news interviews is that a speaker may *formulate* what another has been saying. Formulations generate specific upshots from the talk that are relevant to future actions. For example, a news interviewer may use a formulation of what the interviewee has just said to package a critical point without departing from a stance that is accountably neutral (Greatbatch, 1986). Here is a legal example from the Watergate hearings into President Nixon's involvement in criminal activity. We take it that we do not have any trouble seeing the business Senator Gurney's formulation does.

```
Dean:        . . . I've told you I'm trying to recall. My mind is not a
             tape recorder. It does recall (0.3) impressions of
             conversations very well, and the impression I had was
             that he told- the- he told me that Bob had reported to
             him what I had been doing. That was th- the impression
             that very [clearly came out.
Gurney:                 [In other words, your- your whole thesis on
             saying that the President of the United States knew about
             Watergate on September 15 is purely an impression, there
             isn't a single shred of evidence that came out of this meeting.
             (Edwards and Potter, 1992: 45-6)
```

One of the reasons why formulations are prevalent in institutional settings while being rather rare in informal talk is that they are often designed for overhearers – the jury in a court, the other children in a classroom, the audience in a news interview.

Formulations are a regular feature of focus groups. Moderators are picking out and highlighting what is important as a guide for other group members and to underscore them to the people viewing from behind the one-way mirror and on the tape. Formulating is a delicate task – you are saying what someone else is really saying.

Want to know more?

Heritage and Watson (1980) is the classic paper on this topic. Clayman and Heritage (2002) consider formulations in news interviews.

---

stimulus object; to seeing evaluations as parts of interaction; to seeing evaluations as, in part, produced to counter alternatives.

This is rather abstract so let us consider an example. We have chosen the following as it should be recognizable to most readers (for more details, see Wiggins and Potter, forthcoming). A family meal is going on. Beth is twelve years old and the daughter of Laura. Bill is Beth's uncle. As children do, Beth wants to try some wine.

```
Beth        can I try some ↑wi:ne
Laura       °oh::: (0.2) (↑mm-hm)°
            (2.0)
Beth        don't [↑like red really
Laura             [its very nice:
            (1.0)
Laura       ↑well=
Bill        =how d'you know (0.8) have you ↑ever tried
            it
Beth        I've tried it about a ↑million times
            I hate all red (.) it's too strong
```

Note first how this bit of conversation starts. It starts, as much of real life does, with an action. Beth asks her mother if she can have some wine. Her mother notes the request and agrees (she's a mother, after all – so she does a careful display of deliberation first). She starts to pour Beth some red wine. Now, what happens here is really interesting. Beth rejects the red. But note how she does the rejection: she gives an *evaluation* of the wine. And note also what happens next. We can hear Beth's mother encouraging her to have it. She also does this by giving an *evaluation* of the wine. The point is that evaluations are appearing here as part of the action. They are involved in getting things done rather than presenting abstract judgements.

Now note something else important about this interaction. When Beth turns down the red she does so by making a *subjective evaluation*. That is, she says she *doesn't like* red. Beth's likes are something about her. Now when her mother counters (note the rhetorical organization) she does so with an *objective evaluation*. That is, she specifies some positive quality of the wine: it's *very nice*. Laura is describing something about the wine.

It is easy to blur these different kinds of evaluation together. It is something that attitude researchers often do in their rating scales, which regularly include mixtures of objective and subjective terms. Yet there are important differences between the two. For example, there are different sorts of accountability that come with these two evaluations. In Chapter 1 we emphasized how important accountability is in interaction.

We can see this in the extract above. Beth's uncle Bill challenges her about whether she has ever tried red wine; is her refusal based on experience of not liking it or worry that she will not? Beth is challenged to account for her claim. Note the way she does this. First, she offers an exaggerated gloss on her experience with wine – she has tried it a million times. Second, and more interestingly, she gives a stronger *subjective assessment* of the wine and provides a description that works as an *account* for the assessment.

I <u>hate</u> all ↑red	**Subjective assessment**
it's too <u>strong</u>	**Account for assessment**

There is something really simple yet also really interesting for focus groups going on here. What Beth has done is justify her evaluation with a description of the wine that accounts for it; the wine is 'too strong'. If we are concerned with a product or service, descriptions that are linked to evaluations like this are potentially very useful. Understanding the qualities of things that make them good or bad, will help designers and advertisers. And we will see later in this chapter, and in later chapters, that some of the ways that moderators ask questions are designed to bypass assessments and go directly to the sorts of descriptions that can be used to account for assessments.

Let us pause here for a moment and clarify some terms. We have already noted that focus group researchers have talked about POBAs – perceptions, opinions, beliefs and attitudes. This is a usefully vague term for some purposes. In particular, it highlights a certain kind of objective/subjective contrast. POBAs are all subjective, they are items that people can uniquely provide for themselves. Or, looked at another way, they are items where it is tricky for other people to correct you when you have expressed them. We will be following up these features of POBAs. But we also note that the term can obscure the difference between some things that it can be important to keep separate. In particular, it can be useful to distinguish evaluations (which assess things) from accounts (which justify the assessments), and to distinguish different kinds of evaluations and different kinds of accounts.

In terms of evaluations we have distinguished two broad classes:

1 *Subjective evaluation*: This term is for speakers talking about their personal evaluations or assessments. 'I don't like red' is a subjective evaluation.
2 *Objective evaluation*: This term is for speakers talking about the qualities of things, good or bad. Thus, 'it's very nice' is an objective evaluation.

In terms of accounts, we can usefully distinguish two broad classes.

1 *Epistemic*: Speakers can attend to epistemic issues and questions. How do they know? What is the status of their knowledge? How certain are they? Issues of this kind are often an important part of everyday interaction: are you sure that you are owed 72, or is it 76? – are you sure Peter is an idiot? Important though they are in everyday interaction, they are often just what you don't want in focus groups. This is the kind of thing we talked about in the previous chapter as *account clutter*.

2   *Descriptive*: Speakers can justify their evaluations through the use of descriptions: 'the new tram system in Nottingham is great because it is so smooth and quick'; 'I love my new PC – it's got a really clear screen and a gizmo for editing movies'. These are the kinds of accounts that are often central to focus groups.

We will need to hold these differences in mind as we move on through the book.

Let us end by returning to our more general theme about attitudes and social psychology. What the example we examined in detail illustrated was how drink or indeed any other 'stimulus object' can be negotiated, defined and constructed in talk. This is an ongoing, jointly achieved process. The interesting things to highlight here are the contrast between the traditional social psychology of attitudes and the way evaluations are constructed and used in everyday settings. It is this contrast that helps explain some of the ways that writers on focus groups have considered theoretical notions such as attitudes. In particular, it explains why the broad idea of POBAs might be useful for including attitude notions but not being restricted to them. More interestingly, it also helps in understanding some of the ways that moderators act in groups. It is these things that we now move on to.

Evaluation and attitude in focus groups writing

Writers on focus groups have not failed to show an interest in attitudes. However, they have tended to broaden the social psychological notion. In particular, they have shown little interest in mental processes that they have seen as the province of more academic research in social psychology and other disciplines. And they prefer to loosen the distinctions between attitudes and other related notions – either academic or everyday – rather than to tighten them.

Henderson, for example, describes focus groups as providing:

> end users with appropriate information about target market perceptions, opinions, beliefs and attitudes. (1991: 18)

and, as we have already noted, coins the term POBA. Richard Krueger provides the following definition:

> A focus group is a carefully planned discussion designed to obtain perceptions on a defined area of interest in a permissive, nonthreatening environment. (1994: 6)

Vaughn and colleagues collected a variety of focus group definitions and stated that they usually contain, among others, the following core element:

The goal is to elicit perceptions, feelings, attitudes, and ideas of participants about a selected topic. (1996: 5)

Morgan, finally, prefers in his definition to go:

beyond attitudes and opinions to emphasize learning about participants'
experiences and perspectives. (1997: 20)

In these definitions we can see combined together a large bite from the
psychological thesaurus. As well as perceptions, opinions, beliefs and
attitudes there are also feelings, ideas, experiences and perspectives. This
certainly goes well beyond attitudes and opinions. It is clear that the goal is
not to produce a rigorous technical description of the products of focus
groups but to consider the sorts of terms and descriptions that will
facilitate positive group interaction. Thus Morgan thoughtfully highlights
the value of 'experiences' over 'opinions'. They produce:

a livelier group dynamic – people are more than happy to compare their
different experiences, whereas they might be reluctant to challenge
someone else's opinion. (1997:20)

Furthermore, emphasizing 'perspectives' encourages peopie to think in
more holistic ways and:

brings together attitudes, opinions, and experiences in an effort to find
out not only what participants think about an issue but also how they
think about it and why they think the way they do. (1997:20)

These observations about the product of focus groups emphasize what
works. The test is what will facilitate people's talk rather than the precise
nature of what is produced. They depend on their own common sense, the
common sense of the participants, and that of the readers to sort out what
they are. We understand, or think we do, what perceptions and experiences are, even though if we were asked to be more precise or explicit we
would probably start to get into trouble. Say we were asked to say what a
perception is. We might say it how we *see* things. But that is really just a
paraphrase. We might wonder whether it is some kind of mental picture.
Yet what people offer as perceptions are often conceptual – words and
ideas.

All this seems like trouble. But it is only trouble if we think that the
product of focus groups should be an object such as a set of attitudes. If we
see the language of focus groups to be a practical language we can see that
words like perception and even attitude have an everyday logic that makes
them suitable for certain practical tasks. For focus group moderation the
practical tasks are often rather simple; although no less important for that,
and no less subtle in their achievement. These tasks include encouraging
focus group members to:

- speak about selected objects and ideas;
- stay on topic.

And discouraging members from:

- telling anecdotes and stories;
- filling their talk with account clutter;
- arguing with one another.

Words such as perception and opinion can be central to those practical tasks.

To sum up: writers on focus groups have been vague about what the outcome of the group actually is. This vagueness is an understandable result of the mismatch between the social science origins of focus groups, with its emphasis on technical terms such as attitudes and the practical requirements of group research, which usefully draws on a wide range of non-technical notions. In the absence of an alternative theoretical account for this writing on focus groups has tended to fudge the tension here. However, discursive work provides an account of the role of evaluations in practical settings, and might provide a more coherent theoretical context for understanding interaction in groups and the way they are used in the broader research process.

Now we have cleared the ground a bit let us see how these issues are managed in actual groups. Let us start with moderators' introductions.

Guiding opinion talk in introductions

As we have noted before, when people turn up to take part in a group the chances are that most of them will neither have taken part in one, nor talked to anyone who has nor seen one in operation. If they have heard about focus groups it may well have been in the kind of newspaper reporting that presents them as a slightly devious way for politicians to avoid being accountable to voters.

Newspapers are full of jokes about focus groups, or stories complaining about the use of focus groups in influencing government policy. They often combine a mixture of crude dismissal and rather paranoid image of focus groups as a direct pathway to the nation's consciousness. Here is a not untypical example:

> Focus groups are . . . an abnegation of responsibility for those who rely on them. People in positions of power and influence are paid large sums of money to have the right instincts and the proper judgement. These are the talents they should use to take important decisions. . . . The more focus groups are allowed to influence important decisions, the more

likely the nation's lifeblood will be dominated by the mediocre, the cautious, the safe and the second-rate. (Andrew Neil, *Daily Mail*, 15 Sept. 1997)

Here a well-known commentator depicts focus groups as eating away at the political process.

This combination of clashing images and ignorance means that it is important to start groups off with some general orientation to what is going to happen. And in the course of the group when unfamiliar exercises are started, or trouble arises, moderators may return to general observations about what groups are about and what they are hoping for.

These general introductions do a number of things. We have already noted the way in which they are built to achieve a kind of controlled informality. They are also designed to promote an environment where people can make observations without burying them under account clutter. Part of this may involve the use of the sorts of POBA language we have noted; part of it may involve heading off members' expectations brought from more familiar institutional settings such as schools.

Example introductions

Let us a take an example to illustrate the kind of thing that goes on. This is fairly typical of the different openings we have looked at. It happens to be from a German focus group, but it would not have been out of place elsewhere. It does a lot of important work in a few brief words. We have already looked at some features of it earlier on; let us develop our understanding now.

```
M: Brown    it's just, (.) to find out, (.8)          moves both
            what your gut reactions are, or            hands circling
            what you feel or what you think,           away from his
            you know, (.)                              torso
            uh everybody thinks about the things in
            life in a different way, has,              smiley voice
            things we're talking about, (.8) because
            of that,
            ((clears his throat)) (.)
            it's not like in school or anything like
            that,
```

We can see here moderator Brown starting the group off with a number of POBAesque notions – we have *gut reactions, feelings, what you think*. These are presented as things easy to find out – 'it's *just* to find out' these things. The moderator makes finding these things out a contrast with school, which is thereby presented as more difficult.

Gut reactions is a lovely idiomatic description. It presents the group as looking for something that will emerge organically from within the person. A reaction is something almost chemical or automatic. And moderator Brown enacts what he is going to do in the session by moving both hands in a circling movement away from his torso. He is going to get *out* of the participants' stomachs (figuratively speaking) what is *in* their stomachs.

As we have noted before, things that people 'feel' or 'think' may require less in the way of accounts than knowledge. You can say 'I feel that X is a successful brand' without knowing the actual sales figures. Because feelings and thoughts are reportable in this immediate way without justification they are easily contrasted with the sorts of things that you might be asked to justify in a school lesson.

Here is another example to illustrate the moderator building up these kinds of features at the start of the group. Note the way he presents things as simple, as easy, as POBA based (feelings and thoughts) and about reactions.

```
M: Peter      Its really all about just kind of being
              frank and honest. (0.4) .hh about. (0.6)
              what you fee:l. (0.4) u:m. (0.4) not >at
              any< deep sense or level. 'bout your
              lives: but about. (.) specific things I'm
              going show you. (0.2) >eh< ideas:. (0.2)
              advertising. (0.4) that sort of thing.
              ((lines omitted))
              The ↑way we're gonna look at the
              advertising no:w. (.) e:m. (0.2) is in.
              (.) very. (0.2) (kind) embryonic fo:rm.
              (0.4) It's very early on in its
              development. (.) It's just an idea. (0.2)
              Put together on boards: (0.2) and script.
              (0.4) That's=all. (.) that's the level of
              finish. (.) that we're gonna. (0.2) deal
              with tonight.
              ((lines omitted))
              >but what< we're looking for then is.
              (0.2) a reaction to an idea. (0.2)
              And what's required is >for you< to really
              con- try an' imagine. (0.2) what the
              finished ad will look like. (0.4)
              When you judge it. (0.2) and when you (.)
              evaluate it. (0.4) So you've got to try
              and see beyond (0.2) just a (0.2) piece of
              paper and. (0.2) and the boards that I'm
              going to show you.
              ((lines omitted))
              >Okay. so you. < (.) are you in an imagine
              mo:de. (0.4) >I really want you to think
```

```
about< (0.2) visually what this. (0.2) ad
could be. (0.4) at the end of the day.
(0.2) Okay, so really, (0.2) put your
imagine, (0.2) >your imagine< caps on.
```

At first sight we might wish that moderator Peter had been a bit more precise, a bit more, well *focused*. Yet when we consider how he sets things up we can see that the loose and casual feel disguises some careful work. We have already noted in Chapter 2 the way this general approach with its colloquial and chatty feel generates informality and encourages participation. More specifically of interest to us here is how the task of the group is made easy; it is just about being frank and honest, about what you feel. It is not deep; not something that will require difficult work or things that might be found wanting. They will have to work, but that will be to imagine the finished ad from the notes and sketches that are being shown – *that* is presented as the hard part. All they then need to do to that is report their reaction to it.

Reiterating introductory themes

Moderators can start groups with general statements about what is involved. These have the role of guiding participants to act in ways that are useful to the group. However, predictably such introductory work will not always be sufficient. People forget, or become distracted, or excited. At various points the moderator might need to reiterate the point or pick it out in a different way. For example, a participant might get into trouble in a way that shows that she is focused on publicly justifiable truth and knowledge; this will slow the whole thing down and generate lots of account clutter. If all the members get into this way of acting the group will descend into what we call an *account circus*; a cyclical exchange of increasingly cautious and elaborate accounts.

Here is a simple example. Note the troublesome turn that Anna starts the extract with, and how moderator Tom responds.

```
Anna        >But I don't know, =whether all this is
            true, °I thought, you might know it
            perhaps,°<
→   M: Tom   It doesn't matter, whether anything here
            is true or not true, u:h, (.) if you have
            a view, you can let it out here, this is       Anna
            not a, (.6) kno- knowledge test here,          and some
            or anything like that, (.) you can't win       others
            money either. (.) you'll get your money        laugh
            anyhow. (.8) please fire away, now have
```

	have you any other ideas. about ((the product)) **smiley voice**
Anna	((laughs))

Anna does a number of unhelpful things here. She starts the turn with a disclaimer – saying she does not know. This is account clutter. It is a minor thing on its own. But consider what happens if everyone in the group starts to preface what they say with expressions of caution. If this happens a substantial part of each group will be filled with unhelpful and distracting account clutter.

There is a further element to Anna's contribution. Her provision of a disclaimer goes along with characterizing what she is trying to deliver as the truth (about the effect of some product packaging). Truth and accountability are, of course, bound up together. We have already noted that focus group moderators encourage participants to move away from a truth, knowledge and accountability logic to one based on POBAs. As we have noted, POBAs have the practical feature of minimizing account clutter. If you have an opinion you would not be expected to say how sure you are that you have that opinion! That would sound distinctly odd.

There is a yet further unhelpful element to Anna's contribution, which highlights another crucial feature of POBAs. Note what she does after her disclaimer about the truth of what is being discussed. She asks the moderator! Now this is real trouble. The last thing a moderator wants is to be sucked into the business of the group as a participant. It would be a bit like a television newsreader suddenly being asked her opinion on some political policies in the middle of the news.

The trouble with issues of truth is that they are precisely *not* a matter of individual judgement. The discourse of truth is characterized by universality and general criteria. It is a factual matter whether brand X is the best selling one to Scandinavian women aged over 25; you can be corrected. Moreover, the moderator might well be in as good a position to answer truth related questions as the participants. So the move away from POBAs and towards issues of truth and knowledge risks breaking up the whole social organization of the group. Or, looked at another way, it moves the group members away from a position where they are the unique experts on their own POBAs to one where they may or may not know facts about products or services. It is not surprising, then, that the moderator steps in to deal with this point immediately.

Moderator Tom reasserts what the nature of the focus group is. By stressing that it does not matter if anything is true or not, he is countering Anna's concern with truth. He replaces it with the notion of views, and later ideas. This is done both as something directly, specifically at Anna's turn, but also as a general feature relevant to others in the group.

Note also the way this is managed. What moderator Tom does might be heard as *correcting* group members and expressing his *authority*. As we saw in Chapter 2, these are just the kinds of thing that can discourage participation and make things seem more formal. We can see how moderator Tom presents his emphasis on the members letting their views out by using a slightly humorous manner (note the laughing that accompanies it) and then extends the injunction against seeing what is going on as a knowledge test into a more extreme and playful idea that no one is going to win money as they get paid whatever happens.

The general point here is that focus groups are, typically, novel situations for participants. As such moderators will provide guidance at the start on how to best do the job of being a group member. One aspect of this guidance will be to give answers in the form of POBAs. This is a rather loose category of (broadly) psychological notions; however, the contrasts are spelled out rather more explicitly. Focus groups are *not* about knowledge, truth, tests where you win money for being right and so on. When group members show signs of departing from this guidance in various ways it may be time for the moderator to reassert the centrality of POBAs and remind the members of what they should not be doing.

Evaluations and descriptions

We started this chapter with a discussion of the social psychology of attitudes and how its notions sit rather uneasily with the requirements of focus groups. One of the points we made was that evaluative talk can be done in a number of different ways – sometimes it is offered as a full blown attitude or opinion; at other times evaluations are made indirectly via descriptions which imply evaluations.

Our everyday talk contains an enormously rich set of resources for doing evaluation. This is not surprising as this is something central to us as people, particularly in the consumer culture of the West. Evaluations can be offered as uniquely subjective: 'personally I hated this advert'; or as objective qualities in the world that others might be expected to share: 'the advert was dreadful'. Think how difficult it is in a conversation where someone has just made a strong negative description like this to come in with your own more positive one.

Also, there are ways of making psychological descriptions of things that highlight the speaker or the thing; compare 'I was bored by that advert' with 'that advert is boring'. The former reports a response that is, potentially, individual to the speaker; the latter reports a feature of the advert that might be expected to be recognized by others. It is precisely this richness that the term POBA helps to encompass, and that focus group moderators need to work with to guide effective groups.

In addition to these different ways of marking evaluation, people can offer descriptions of things that categorize them, or highlight some of their features. This car styling is 'modern' or 'classic' or 'relaxed'. In some circumstances these might be treated as evaluative, in others they might be complementary descriptions offered by different speakers.

There may be a number of reasons why moderators may encourage participants to provide more evaluative contributions or ones that provides descriptions that are not directly evaluative. Some of these relate to the reason the specific focus group is being run in the first place. However, others relate to issues of interaction and the way focus groups are made manageable and informative. Let us start with a consideration of the pros and cons of practices that require evaluations before considering practices that require descriptions.

Conversation Box 4.2
Offering candidate answers

Information seeking is a commonplace activity and we use a variety of strategies to elicit information from one another. One strategy involves incorporating a candidate answer in a query. Anita Pomerantz (1988) has shown that supplying a model answer is useful when a speaker wants to guide, direct or assist a respondent in providing particular information. Take the following:

```
Are you going to be here for awhile?
You're feeding him on Cow and Gate Premium?
Was Tom home from school ill today?
```

In each case the question provides guidance as to the appropriate answer, or what the answer is that the questioner expects.

When seeking information we have options as to how much or how little guidance we give a recipient with respect to what information is relevant. This is useful if we would like to elicit particular information in an efficient way. And it is useful when we anticipate or observe the recipient having difficulty giving a satisfactory answer without a model. In short, offering a candidate answer is functional whenever a speaker has a reason to guide the recipient of her or his query in a particular way.

Pomerantz notes that candidate answers are often provided when speakers are being friendly or cooperative. They tend to be *affiliative*. This is a useful feature for focus groups where the moderator is trying to shape participants' responses while sustaining a welcoming and supportive environment.

Want to know more?

Pomerantz (1988) is the classic paper on information seeking and candidate answers.

Evaluation

If we consider the research on the way people make evaluations in everyday settings there is a very basic pattern. Anita Pomerantz (1984) has shown that when one speaker offers an evaluation of something – a meal, a film, the weather, whatever – the person they are talking to will, typically and very regularly, offer an evaluation of their own. Indeed, if they do not offer one this will often be taken as a *disagreement* with what came before.

When people come to take part in focus groups they are aware that it is a special situation – it is not the same as sitting round in the pub chatting or arguing over dinner. And we have noted that the moderator puts quite a lot of work into building this special nature of what will go on. However, people bring with them a whole package of everyday expectations and practices. Expectations about evaluations is one of the aspects that is not easily abandoned, and these expectations can be *exploited* by moderators. When one participant is encouraged to give an evaluation other participants often offer their own evaluations. That is, eliciting one evaluation from an individual can be an indirect technique for eliciting a number of evaluations from other individuals.

Let us illustrate this with an example. It is a slightly complex one, but we will use it to illustrate a further point, so stay with us. This extract comes from a group discussing advertising ideas for a hair shampoo. The participants have watched a preliminary version of the advert on video that shows an image of a pregnant woman.

```
Julie         °It° doesn't tell you how it's working.
              (.)
Alexis        hm mm.
Bea           No:,=
Alexis        =No
Bea           °That's right.° (0.2) But that's, (.)
              (from) the image that is given.=
→ M: Martha   =So what (0.2) what's, (0.2) what's the      Moderator
              pregnant >(woman)< =you didn't like, (0.6)   Martha
              [°the pregnant (one >didn't work<)]          addresses
                                                           Susan
Susan         [Oh no I'm (.) I-              ] think
              >totally< u:sed, (.) the, (0.2) image of     hesitantly
              (the) pregnant women, (.) and, (0.2) you
              know the=the mothers h=hholding, (0.4) the
              hands=
Some          =°hm°=
Susan         =it's >so overused< it's (.)                 Susan
              bo[ ring re ]ally                            evaluates
?               [ >hm mm, < ]
```

```
Susan       It could be. (0.2) one of. (0.6)           hesitantly
            anything [(really)]
Bea                  [It's    ] a bit cheap really     second
            [°(sometimes)°]                            evaluation
Susan       [yea::h.      ] (0.2) u:hm, (1.0) just a
            bit of personal >(xxx) isn't it because. <
            (0.2) some of the others liked.[that  ]
M: Karen                                   [hm mm.]
Susan       that image (.) °with the° woman with just   Bea and Susan
            (both of the-) (0.2) .hh pregnant woman      start to laugh
            >°(I don't know)°<
```

This is a lively group. Moderator Karen works to break into the talk as the participants discuss the advert they have been shown, rather like marketing experts discussing a brand image. She jumps in very quickly after Bea's point about the image. Having got a toehold in the interaction, she recycles the start of her question, working more slowly now she has the group's attention. She moves things away from abstract brand talk about advertising images to the participants' personal judgements. She starts this off by eliciting a specific evaluation from an individual, Susan, who has already provided comments that suggest her view.

There are two features of this interaction we want to highlight. First, when Susan comes in with her evaluation she does not just offer the assessment ('I don't like pictures of pregnant women') she provides *accounts* for this assessment – they are 'overused', 'boring', 'could be anything'. Second, after Susan has offered her evaluation, Bea follows it up with a *second* evaluation: 'it's a bit cheap'. Bea has not been directly asked her view (note that Susan was picked out in the moderator's question). Just as in everyday conversation, one evaluation leads to another.

There are costs and benefits for moderators when they elicit evaluations in this way. On the benefit side, eliciting evaluations:

- (obviously) provides evaluations. Positive and negative views of adverts, services and so on may be one of the focus group goals;
- generates rich and lively talk among participants. One participant's evaluation leads to another, and possibly further members join in;
- generates accounts for evaluations. These in themselves may satisfy the research goals – the advertiser may find it helpful to discover that people find images of pregnancy 'overused'.

There are costs, however, in eliciting evaluation. In particular, eliciting evaluation may:

- generate rather complicated interaction that may be hard to write up in a report and hard to appreciate while watching;

- generate interaction that is hard to direct as the turn organization is from participant to participant rather than having the interaction work through the moderator;
- generate unhelpful epistemic accounting, swamping assessments and descriptive accounts with long-winded and distracting account clutter.

For these reasons, while most focus groups involve some requests for evaluations, they are rarely the only thing that is required. Instead focus groups often mix requests for evaluations with the elicitation of descriptions. The two together complement one another and provide more information than one or other alone.

Descriptions

Earlier in the chapter we considered Zanna and Rempel's definition of attitudes. One of its features is to draw attention to the role of categorization. Making an evaluation will involve categorizing something in a particular way. From our perspective it is useful to see categorizations as parts of practices of evaluation rather than pieces of cognitive processing. We have also noted something more specific than that. Descriptive categorizations often appear as accounts for evaluations. Schematically, using examples from above:

Evaluation	**Account**
I hate all red	it's too strong
I don't like the pregnant woman image	it's overused.

One of the things that we see in focus groups is very neat. Moderators regularly ask questions that attempt to get the participants to deliver the sorts of descriptive accounts that they would give for evaluations, without delivering the evaluations themselves. The advantage of this is that the sorts of pressures to follow assessments with agreements that Anita Pomerantz (1984) has identified in everyday conversation, and we saw in our previous focus group extract, are lessened. For example, rather than asking participants to evaluate some product or service, they might be asked what kind of thing that product or service is. This may throw important light on the focus group topic, and so may be valuable in its own right. However, and equally importantly, it may break up the complex pressures that come with assessment talk. Asking for descriptive accounts can be a way of simplifying the talk, and gaining more control of the interaction.

Let's take an example to illustrate this in action. In the following extract we can see the moderator switching to a questioning mode that asks for descriptions rather than evaluations. This switch is not haphazardly placed

– it happens just where the group is getting rather complex and where participants are starting to offer accounts and qualifications on what they are saying.

It comes from a group concerned with cars and their interior detailing. At the point where the extract starts the participants have agreed that one of the colourful fabric swatches on display is not suitable for them; it seems to be designed for young people rather than families. Here, however, Saul starts to change and suggest that the colours are a refreshing contrast to 'grey and flannel' and, significantly, that it is hard to assess car fabrics when they are not in the car.

Saul	=I think it's nice to get awa:y (>if you see<) from the slate grey and flannels (.) they look like (they got here) (.) °can we.° =	
Colin	= °hm° =	
Saul	=And. (.) it's very hard to. (.) just: see it's like choosing a piece of wallpaper =	
Andy	ye:[ah,]	
Saul	[or (xxx)] [I mean if you see] (it spread out it's easier to) imagine in the vehicle	
Alan	[((inaudible))]	
M: Mike	>hm hm. hm mm.<	starts to intervene
Saul	In some ways it's (xxxxx) better than: (.) than- than I think it could. (.) it could=>it could [look quite nice<]	
Alan	[>might< be o↑kay=°yeah.°] ((lines omitted))	
M: Mike	The longer you're looking at it you're warming up to=	further intervention
Saul	=yeah! (.) a little bit	
Gisa	>(If it's just), discreetly u:sed [(y'know not the whole (.) thing=and.)]	
Saul	[(depends how you choose yeah)]	
Carl	I think it's a matter of >sitting in the car anyway.<=one=once they're in the car you probably say 'Oh yeah [that's quite nice']	
→ M: Mike	[(xxxxxx)] (.) (this is it) (.) this is. (.)	further intervention
Brian	Loud	
M: Jeff	Lou:d. (0.6)	
Carl	>(true)<=	

```
M: Mike      =< Younger > person's er (0.2) y'know
              < immature. > (.)
```

The first thing to note about the initial section of this extract is that Saul and others are starting to qualify their prior assessments of the fabric and, more importantly, starting to suggest that the whole task (of commenting on fabrics out of context) is a problem. Moderator Mike starts to intervene with some quick 'hm mm.'s' which show some impatience and implies that they should move on. Saul, however, continues to qualify his earlier evaluation. At this point Mike the moderator comes in again, in a slight overlap that suggests further impatience. Nevertheless, Saul and Carl continue to provide qualified evaluations that focus on the difficulty of the task.

So far the interaction has not been ideal, then. On the one hand, it has generated some evaluations of the fabrics, which is a good thing. On the other, it has got side tracked on to problems with the task and the participants have not responded to the moderator's so far rather indirect attempts to move things on. It is definitely not a good thing for the moderator when participants start to question the value of tasks they have been set! Nevertheless, it is what happens now that we are most interested in. The moderator changes the questioning mode from a request for *evaluations* to one that requires *descriptions* of the fabric. This takes the form of a quick fire sentence completion task: 'this is . . .', where a participant fills in a quality or characteristic. In this case Brian fills in this quality as 'loud' and Moderator Mike repeats 'loud' to show he has heard it, and that it is the right kind of thing.

As we will see in the next chapter, this pattern of interaction is very common in focus groups. Often it can include a number of group members in turn. Schematically it will look like this:

Moderator	Asks for description	**Directly or indirectly**
Member 1	Provides description	**Typically one or two words**
Moderator	Repeats description	**May then orient to further members**
Member 2	Provides further description	
Moderator	Repeats description	**And so on . . .**

There are three points to highlight about this pattern of interaction for our current interests.

- First, it concentrates on descriptions rather than evaluations. These descriptions may be qualities or aspects of products.

- Second, it is talk that participants typically produce without further accounts or qualifications. Indeed, it is the kind of talk that is used to account for evaluations.
- Third, it is talk that goes via the moderator who provides a repeat of each description.

The benefit of eliciting descriptions such as these directly, is that a variety of different contributions can be generated without the participants needing to orient to conflict between different assessments. They can sit unchallenged next to each other, perhaps being treatable as complementary aspects of one phenomenon, different facets of a car's colour scheme for example. A feature of asking for descriptions like this is that the moderator is much more guiding and controlling. This can be a good thing, and can break up interaction whose complexity and trajectory has become hard to manage; however, it is hard work for a moderator to sustain for a long period of time and it starts to undermine one of the valued features of focus groups, that contributions are offered spontaneously.

SUMMARY

There is a tension in focus group research between the social science origins of groups and the modern practice of focus group research. The tension arises in particular as a consequence of the limitations of the traditional social science notion of attitudes for a research technique that emphasizes interaction. This tension is hidden by notions such as POBAs – perceptions, opinions, beliefs, and attitudes – which blur together a range of different notions. Although it appears less technical this range of notions captures better the complicated ways in which people talk in everyday settings.

Moderators may encourage POBA talk in their introductions to focus groups. They may also encourage participants to continue talking in POBAs in the course of groups, particularly if participants drift into talking about knowledge, facts or truth.

POBA talk has a number of features that makes it ideal for focus groups. POBAs:

- are directly and immediately available to the speaker rather than identified through inference (so they are objects that speakers can be expected to have no problem in generating);
- may be individual rather than consensual (everyone may have their own views or opinions);
- should be available to all groups members (not just the educated, clever or sophisticated);

- are things that the participants are more expert in than the moderator (each participant will be in the best position to know his or her own views).

Although POBA talk is fundamental to focus groups, it is often supplemented by other kinds of talk. It is useful to distinguish between:

- subjective evaluations ('I don't like red wine');
- objective evaluations ('red wine is nice');
- epistemic accounts ('I am not an expert on red wine');
- descriptive accounts ('this red wine is mellow').

Although evaluations are central to POBAs, epistemic and descriptive accounts do not necessarily take a POBA form. One common moderator practice is to ask questions designed to access descriptive accounts directly. This can have the double advantage of both getting at descriptive accounts without the evaluations that can cause interactional complications and also allowing the moderator to have more control over the interaction. The disadvantage is that the degree of control may discourage a range of interesting contributions from participants. For this reason it is unlikely that a good focus group will be made up entirely of descriptive questions; more likely it will have alternating phases of evaluative and descriptive questions.

TURNING PRACTICES INTO STRATEGIES

STRATEGY ONE
Use an introduction that makes clear that the aim is not to find out how much participants actually know about a product. Make it clear that you are after people's POBAs. Emphasize the likelihood and acceptability of them producing different POBAs.

STRATEGY TWO
Monitor carefully for breakdowns where participants start to make knowledge and truth claims, and become concerned with evidence and the moderator's own knowledge. Reiterate the focus on POBAs as needed.

STRATEGY THREE
When talk is slow moving or when group members appear uninvolved ask for evaluations. This will lead to more lively talk with accounts and second assessments. This strategy is particularly good when a range of different views is not required. It may be hard to control and poor at allowing minority views to flourish.

STRATEGY FOUR
When talk has been lively and hard to follow or control ask for descriptions. This will lead to short contributions and is likely to promote variety. It will also provide a way of exerting more control over the trajectory of the group.

5 Producing Useful Opinions

At the start of Chapter 3 we noted that there is a tension in focus group interaction between freedom and determinism. It shares this with a number of other group settings. For example, Derek Edwards and Neill Mercer (1987) studied interaction in science classrooms. One of the striking things they found was that teachers placed a lot of stress on the pupils discovering facts for themselves using experiments. Yet when they looked closely at video records of the lessons they found the teachers were doing what the researchers called 'cued elicitation'. That is, they were using a whole range of indirect techniques to lead pupils to the right answers. These things included:

* using gestures to indicate correct responses;
* using silence to discourage wrong answers while encouraging right answers;
* paraphrasing what the pupils said to bring them close to correct responses;
* summarizing events to reconstruct them as having been discovered by pupils.

In effect, the lessons were suffused with a persistent but indirect teacher choreography as they worked to get the required outcomes out of children. At the same time, they were constructing what went on as a product of the pupils themselves. Edwards and Mercer were not criticizing these practices. Rather, they were suggesting that this tension is an intrinsic and creative part of running good lessons.

Focus groups present a very similar problem of choreography. The moderator needs to lead the group members to the correct answer (or at least answers that are appropriate and useful) while all the time presenting it as something arrived at by the members themselves. The art of this when it is working well is that the focus group produces just the right sorts of outcomes; and yet it does this in a way that feels fluid, relaxed and open-ended. The moderator controls the interaction without being heavy handed and with as little overt direction as possible. This is a mixture of encouraging participants to provide responses of the right kind, and discouraging irrelevant material such as academic discussions or long personal narratives. It is hard work; but should appear effortless.

The special nature of focus groups and their outcome requires a special set of techniques. In the course of this book we have been noting research by discursive psychologists and conversation analysts on the way evaluations are produced in interaction. This work shows the way that evaluations are produced to perform *actions* (Potter, 1998a) and where one evaluation has been produced other speakers typically offer their own evaluation (Pomerantz, 1984). It also shows that evaluations are typically produced in the context of at least potential *argument* (Billig, 1991, 1996) and providing an evaluation *for* something is, often, implicitly providing an evaluation *against* something else (Billig, 1988). Broadly speaking, it is better to treat evaluative talk in terms of its role in interaction rather than trying to characterize it using notions such as attitudes and opinions.

This active and rhetorical feature of opinion talk is one of the reasons why focus groups can be such an effective research technique. Yet it presents a challenge for moderators. They have to produce relatively freestanding packages of opinions out of the active and argumentative interaction. There are, therefore, two levels of choreography that the moderator needs to attend to. At the more general level, the moderator needs to be able to head off interaction that is irrelevant and guide the participants into making spontaneous POBA style talk. At a more specific level, he or she needs to be able to generate POBAs as freestanding packages relatively disengaged from the current interaction.

It is worth reminding ourselves at this point of one of the key features that distinguishes market research focus groups from those used for social science questions. In market research focus groups the findings are not clearly separate from the group interaction. Instead, the interaction, in an important sense, *is* the findings. It is what is seen through the one-way mirror and it makes up the video that is a major product of the group. This means that moderator techniques for generating spontaneity and constructing opinion packages are not just there to make the job of report writing simpler; they guide the interaction in a way that makes the opinions, beliefs and attitudes clearly *visible*. The better the production of visibility the more valuable to the advertisers or product designers will be viewing the group. These skills are crucial to running good groups.

This chapter will describe a number of practices that moderators can employ to elicit good answers in a way that appears spontaneous. In particular, it will focus on:

- openings and their encouragement of spontaneity;
- shaping answers by using candidate formats and candidate answers;
- stripping off irrelevant features using repeat receipts;
- using a whiteboard;
- moderator correction of different kinds.

Spontaneity and group openings

As in previous chapters, let us start by considering moderator openings. How are issues of spontaneity and the nature of what participants should produce to be addressed? The answer is that moderators develop two simultaneous strands of thinking. One strand constructs what participants will do in the group as natural, non-demanding, and rather like a version of what they might do anyway. Moderators can build a contrast between knowledge that might be taxing and got wrong, with POBAs that are already there in the top of their heads, or in their stomachs, and are therefore easy to produce. The other strand constructs, ever so gently, the sort of natural, easy thing that participants ought produce. It is not just anything; it is opinions or perceptions. And it is not *just* opinions; it is reasons, the *descriptive accounts* for those opinions.

Let us take a series of examples to flesh this out. We have indicated sections where moderators are suggesting how open the group will be, and sections where they are directing participants on how to act. Here is a fragment from an opening.

```
M: Sandy   I don't want to ↑interro↓gate, and          open
           I certainly don't want to ↑test ↓you. (.)    open
           and
           it's not about ↑know↓ledge,                  open
           but about o↑pin↓ions,                        directing
           >you just always say, whatever comes to      open
           mind, (.)and there are<
           no, (.) right or wrong answers.              open
```

This is a characteristic piece. Some version of this is typically present in openings of market research focus groups. Note the contrast – the moderator starts with what she is *not* going to do, that is interrogate or test the participants. By doing this she identifies potential fears that they might have and counters them. Interrogation and tests are familiar negative situations involving *knowledge*. What Sandy wants from the group, however, is not knowledge – it is *opinions*. The term 'opinions' is then unpacked as saying whatever comes to mind with no right or wrong answers. That is, opinions are *made into* this free and obvious thing to say.

Let us note two further features of this piece. First, it provides a nice reminder that the moderator's talk is carefully recipient designed. It is made to be clearly understandable. This can be seen here with the exaggerated intonational contours on the key words 'interrogate', 'test', 'knowledge' and 'opinions'. Also, its structure is clearly formatted with repeated phrases to make the contrast as clear as possible. The moderator is making sure the participants get the point. Indeed, it is not dissimilar to some of the patterns that conversation analysts such as John Heritage and David Greatbatch (1986) have identified in political speeches that generate applause. And this analogy is a useful one as the start of the group is a bit like a speech – the moderator will speak for an extended period and therefore needs to both be clear and keep the member's attention.

The second point brings us back directly to the topic of the chapter. The construction here emphasizes the negative and coercive things that will not be done. It offers instead a situation where members can just say whatever comes to mind. That is a powerful image of freedom. Yet at the same time it provides a specific output that is required: the participants should be providing opinions. However open-ended and self-directed they are going to be in the group, opinions are what are required!

In this example we can see the moderator emphasizing the simplicity of what will go on.

```
M: Ewan    Its really all about just kind of being      open/
           frank and honest.                            direct
           (0.4) .hh
           about. (0.6) what you fee:l.                 directing
           (0.4) u:m. (0.4)
           not > at any < deep sense or level. 'bout    open
           your lives: but about. (.) specific things
           I'm going show you. (0.2) > eh < ideas:.
           (0.2) advertising. (0.4) that sort of
           thing.
```

It is *all about just* being *frank* and *honest*. This is an easy thing. The *just* emphasizes that. It implies that there will be no reasoning or work needed – *just* disclosure. This is coupled with the standard POBA term – in this case it is *feel*. Again, feelings are things that a person can have that do not imply they should be correct or satisfy public criteria.

The contrast here is not school but *deep level* revelations. The moderator is probably managing one of the possible implications of asking people to be frank and honest – which is that they may have something to be deceitful or dishonest about. And this is one of the anxieties that people may have about social researchers, including market researchers; that they may be trying to delve into secret desires or unstated wishes. The moderator does a bit of work to head this off.

The general point, though, is that what will go on is simple, but it is specific – feelings about advertising ideas. The delivery makes it seem unconstrained. The moderator in the next extract also combines an expression of openness with some rather specific guidance.

```
M: Lucy      > So I don't really mind what you say < (.)      open
             Having ↑said that. (1.0) .hhh It's very          directing
             ea:sy > if you see < something you haven't
             seen before > to say <
             Ooh hate that. (.) I hate that.
             At > which point (.) there's no point <
             discussing it any fur↓ther. (.)
             So I a:sk you to not use the words I hate
             that. (.) or the words (.) I love that.
             (0.2) .hh until we're way down the line
             (.) becau:se, (1.0) > do you see what I
             mean = once you start saying you hate
             something < (0.2) then, (0.4) > everyone'll
             get v- very negative <
```

The tension here should not be overstated. The moderator is stressing her general openness to the participants but qualifying it with some specific things that will cause problems. She is trying to head off participants making strong claims that may inhibit the others, although couched in a loose gloss about things getting 'very negative'. Here is one final example. The point to notice again is how the moderator's directive move is couched in terms of a stress on openness.

```
M: Chris     You > don't < have to say nice things to     open
             keep me hap↓py. (0.2)
             As long as you explain why you have a        directing
             point of view that's all that matters = I
             mean I-I °clearly.° (0.2) I can't go back
             to my clients and say, (0.4) .hh I spoke
             > to these < eight people thought 'all the
             ideas were (0.2) a:bsolute rubbish' (.) if
             I haven't got (.) some kind of
             justification.
```

Moderator Chris here starts off by emphasizing the *lack* of constraints on the group members. They don't need to say nice things to keep him happy. But he goes on to indirectly produce a constraint – they need to provide a justification for their views. They will not only need to offer evaluations but also give their reasons for those evaluations. These are the descriptive accounts that we talked about in the previous chapter. There is a delicately managed guidance to the participants as part of an emphasis on openness.

The general point here is a simple one. On the one hand, moderators stress openness and spontaneity in their introductions. They construct focus groups as places of openness rather than constraint, where participants will do something they will find very simple. On the other, they provide a range of specific guidance as to what is wanted:

- POBA talk;
- justifications of evaluations;
- honesty and directness;
- a focus on advertising ideas or whatever the group topic is.

And what is not wanted:

- answers that can be right or wrong;
- strong evaluations;
- things said just to keep the moderator happy.

Having started with introductions we will move on to consider some of the other ways in which moderators shape the activities of the group members and bring them into line with what is required.

Shaping the future and repairing the past

There is a simple sense in which there are two places to effect something that a participant has said. The moderator can do something *before* what is said or *after*. They can shape the future or they can repair the past. And there is a range of ways of doing either. In most cases it will be better to shape the future, as repair is a pretty delicate thing to do. However, there is often no choice. Furthermore, moderators' repairs serve a dual role. They address inadequacies with a specific contribution and they educate the group as to what the right thing to do is. It is worth reminding ourselves yet again that for the participants the focus group is a novel setting and they will most likely be attending closely so they can learn what is appropriate and what is not.

We will start by considering how information-seekers guide recipients in such a way as to elicit specific information or a particular style of response. We will then consider the phenomenon of repair – that is, error-correction and the modification of what is said in everyday talk.

Shaping future answers

Information seeking is a commonplace mundane activity. We do it day in and day out, as we make arrangements, ask about our friend's health, gossip, argue and do our jobs. There is a wide variety of different practices for eliciting information, and what will be used in any given case will depend on a number of different considerations. We have already considered the general class of questions and the specific practice of fishing in Chapter 3. In this chapter the focus will be on the way questions can be used to give cues and hints in order to direct the recipient to a particular answer or a particular style of answer.

More specifically we will concentrate on two techniques. The first involves incorporating *candidate formats* and/or *candidate answers* as parts of elaborate questions. In offering a candidate answer the moderator attempts to lead the respondent to provide particular information. Candidate answers also allow the moderator to display their knowledge of, and familiarity with, the focus group situation. Candidate formats are similar, but only provide the format of the answer that is required, without giving any specific examples. The second technique involves the repeating of a key word from the participant's answer. We have already encountered this in the previous chapter. The focus here will be on the shaping role of such *repeat receipts*. Moderator responses of this kind model the appropriate way for participants to answer.

There is a dilemma here; and that is why moderators use rather direct techniques to shape answers. As we have already noted in Chapter 3, moderators need to be careful with respect to their expertise. They can be experts on the process – they are market researchers after all, who ought to know how focus groups operate. However, if they become seen as experts on the products or services that are the topic of the group then all kinds of troubling things happen. Participants may be inhibited in giving their views as they will be amateurs compared with the moderator. They may ask the moderator questions. They may submerge their responses in a sea of qualifying account clutter. This leaves the moderator with a tricky and important task. They need to be a market research expert, but naïve with respect to the nature of the product. This makes it particularly tricky to shape appropriate responses. The risk is that when the moderator shapes a response it will suggest that the participant has misunderstood the product, and this, in turn, will display the wrong kind of expertise by the moderator. The beauty of the practices of candidate answers and repeat receipts is that they manage this dilemma in an indirect way.

Candidate answers

In Chapter 3 we described the way moderators build elaborate questions and what their role is. These elaborate questions add qualifying components and are often delivered in a somewhat hesitant manner. This works as a display of informality and to help secure participation. As we return to elaborate questions our focus will be on the way they incorporate candidate answers. The value of candidate answers is that they provide a guide or format for appropriate responses. There are two dangers in using candidate answers in this way. First, they may be treated as a closed list of options. This will prevent the moderator getting at the range of possible POBAs and descriptive accounts that are needed for a good group. Second, they may be treated as a display of moderator expertise about the product or service. This will lead to all the troubles noted above when the moderator is treated as knowledgeable. So the art is to offer the candidates in a way that manages these two dangers. Let's now look at how this is done.

The following extract comes from a group concerned with advertising in general. We have chosen it to show the shaping feature of elaborate questions. Wim has offered a negative comment about washing powder advertising. However, rather than providing a support for this comment, he starts to make observations about advertising people and their jobs. This is just the kind of thing that you don't want as a moderator – participants are almost always discouraged from playing at marketing experts. This happens here as moderator Karl interrupts Wim and addresses him with an elaborate question which we have arrowed.

```
     Wim          Advertising for washing powder is, is the
                  most deadly. I, (.9) always try then to
                  imagine, what sort of person can think up
                  something ↑like ↓this
     Alan         ((laughs))
     Wim          although perhaps for washing powder
                  itself, (.) someho:w (.7) perhaps
                  I couldn't come up with anything better      smiley voice
                  either.
                  (.9) It is [(°xxxxxxxxxxxxxxxxxx°)]
→    M: Karl             [ And if you see such an  ] ad,
                  (.) uh how do you then react to it           candidate
                  e↑motionally,                                format
                  well do you get annoyed about it or do you   candidate
                  say                                          answer 1
                  Hu, hu, what total rubbish that ↑is (.)      candidate
                  .hh or, (.) how, u:h how do you yourself     answer 2
                  react ↑to ↓it
     Wim          Yes, sometimes I get (°really°) annoyed.
                  (.) Then I say emphatically, well, (.8)
                  yes, this can't be true (that's complete
                  rubbish) (1.2) whatever,
```

After Wim's inadequate answer Moderator Karl pursues a *good* answer by asking a complex follow-up question. This has a form typical of elaborate questions:

- Question including candidate format
- Candidate answer 1
- Candidate answer 2
- Reiteration of question

In this case there are two candidate answers and a closing reiteration. As we noted in Chapter 3, further elaboration could have been introduced by providing question reformulations after the initial question and further candidate answers. The two candidate answers offered here are:

`you get annoyed about it`

and

`you say hu hu what total rubbish that is.`

Both of these candidates are negative, probably picking up from the general negative 'deadly' picture of washing powder ads that has been offered earlier. But in this case the question coaches POBAs (note the stress and intonation on the word 'emotionally') as the proper *format* of answer. And the candidates offer the participant a gloss on his emotional state – 'annoyed' – or the sort of words that someone might say: 'total rubbish'.

It is clear how this works as coaching. The question and candidate answers work together to provide a template for the appropriate response. They provide a snapshot picture of what a good answer would be. This can be used as a model both by Wim who has been addressed and other members listening.

How does the moderator prevent this becoming an option list and a display of dangerous knowledge about soap commercials? There are several detailed features of the delivery that head off the candidates becoming an option list.

First, and most prominently, the intonation is used to mark it off as an incomplete list. When people offer complete lists, in political speeches for example, they typically deliver the last item with a downward intonation. In this case the second and last item finishes with a noticeable upward intonation: 'what total rubbish that ↑is'.

A second feature of the delivery is the opening of a further list item that is not completed. Following the second candidate the moderator continues with 'or' suggesting that a third candidate is to come; but he does not go on to specify it. Again this is a simple way of showing that what is offered is not a complete option list.

A third feature to note is the hesitancy of the delivery. Note the questioning intonation coupled with the 'uh' near the start and then the stuttering start to the final reiteration of the question: '.hh or, (.) how, u:h how . . .'. The questions and options are constructed as tentative. This is ideal for working against the idea that the moderator knows all about the product and the questions are a test for the participants. Part of the beauty is that it utilizes something that is easy to do, which is to be a bit tentative, to make things up as you go along. In incorporating a candidate answer in his question *and* in simultaneously providing an array of question components presented in a tentative manner, the moderator displays both a degree of knowledge of the participant's reaction to adverts for washing powder, *and* his own uncertainty about whether the candidate answer leads the participant in the right direction.

There is a bit of a balancing act going on. The aim will be to display expertise on group process and what kind of things clients will want, but to be something of an amateur on the qualities of the product, policy or service that the group is concerned with. The participants need to be made the real experts in their own views and feelings. What we have illustrated here is the skill that the moderator needs to construct questions in a way that supports this balance.

The next section will consider another technique that moderators use to shape participants' responses into the required forms, namely repeat receipts. It will also illustrate the way these are combined with candidate answers, and therefore provide further examples of candidate answers in practice.

Repeat receipts

We have already encountered repeat receipts in Chapter 4 where we considered their role in eliciting brief descriptions and avoiding some of the over-lively interaction that can come with evaluations and their justifications. Here we consider a number of further interactional features of repeat receipts and in particular the way in which they can be used to shape the responses that group members give. Repeat receipts have a powerful double feature. On the one hand, they provide a model for future answers. On the other, they avoid the moderator having to be an authority on the topic under discussion.

Receipts in other settings

Let us step back a bit to think about this by considering the way information is responded to in other settings. As John Heritage (1984b) has shown, when people are told stories or items of news in everyday settings they typically provide news receipts such as 'oh' or 'did she?' or offer assessments such as 'that's good'. However, these are rare in focus groups, which are much more like news interviews, which also contain few explicit news receipts. You only have to watch an evening of television news and look for a news interviewer saying 'oh really' or something similar. It is very unusual. Yet, as Heritage along with David Greatbatch (1986) show, news interviewers regularly *formulate* the contributions of interviewees: 'so you are saying that the economy is shaky'.

We can start to make sense of this by considering the different particip-ant roles or, as conversation analysts put it, the different *footings* of people receiving news in everyday and news settings. If our friend tells us that she has passed an important exam we may reply 'oh that's great'. The 'oh' receipt marks what Heritage calls a 'change of state' that is, it shows that the news is really newsworthy (that we had not already heard it). The evaluation marks our personal stance to it. However, consider the news interviewer. They are doing the interview for an overhearing or viewing audience. If they ask the interviewee a question and get an answer the issue is not whether it is news to them (they may have been well briefed beforehand, after all), it is whether it will be news to the audience. The interviewer is not the person who the answer is meant for. Hence the lack of news receipts. Likewise with evaluations. The news interviewer's role is not to evaluate the answers but to elicit them for the audience to evaluate. Formulations, however, are ways of packaging, clarifying and reordering what the interviewee has said for the audience, or to build for a further question.

Receipts in focus groups

This idea of a participant role, or footing, is important in focus groups. By avoiding news receipts the moderator presents him or herself as not the final recipient of the information but as someone who is generating information for some other party (a company, organization or political party). Crucially, they do not present themselves as changing their knowl-edge state, as starting to know more about the product, as developing an *expertise* that might lead them to assess members' contributions. Nor are formulations very common. Although there is an overhearing audience (behind the one-way mirror and watching the video) formulations are probably too time consuming where there is a group of five or more people all offering POBAs. Overwhelmingly the solution that moderators use is the repeat receipt.

Let us illustrate this with an example. This involves a group on the design of vans. They are in a large hall where they have been considering actual vans as well as pictures of vans. This sequence comes after an exercise where group members have selected the favourite vans from a set of cut out pictures and started to offer general things that they liked and disliked about them.

<pre>
  →   M: Yvonne ↑What dyou want people to th<u>ink</u> ↓when they
                 see you driving around in your van.
                 (2.0)
      Brian   It's a nice ↑van=
      Dave   =get out the way
                 ((laughter))
  →   M: Yvonne Yeah, it's a nice van. (0.6)   repeat receipt
                 >so the less< Postman Pat the better (.) gestures for
                 so what dyou want. (0.2)   quiet
                 Hang on. Shhhh. (0.2)
                 the less Postman Pat the better (.) what
                 dyou want.
                 (1.0)
      Diana   <u>Not</u>, to look like a Noddy ca:r,
      M: Yvonne Yeah?
      Diana   Just <u>not</u> to look ridiculous.
                 <u>not</u> to look like a Noddy car=
                 to look more like a car. =
                 its like pic five it looks a lot more like
                 a car in the fr<u>o:nt</u>.
                 (0.6)
  →   M: Yvonne What do you think=what sort of wo:rds   request for
                 would you use to describe >if it was your< description
                 id<u>ea</u>l van. (.) yeah? (.) .hh and it was
                 less, (.) less Noddy>like< if you like.
                 (0.2)
                 What sort of <u>words</u> would you use to   reiteration
                 describe the ideal=   reiteration
                 what [would it look] like
      Graham   [Stylish   ]
  →   M: Yvonne Stylish,   repeat receipt
                 (1.0)   moderator
                                                           gestures for
                                                           more
      Diana   Practical.
  →   M: Yvonne Practical, what else.
                 (1.0)   snaps finger
                 What would your ideal l<u>oo</u>k like. (1.0) points at Keith
                 °(say about you (0.2) >and< your company)°
      Keith   A bit sporty?
      Steve   Sma:rt
  →   M: Yvonne A bit spor↑ty (0.2) ↑smart   repeat receipt
                 (1.0)   scans group
      M: Yvonne Okay, what about number s<u>ix</u>. (0.2) Who
                 chose number s<u>ix</u>.
</pre>

This type of interaction is typical of focus groups. It is worth considering in a bit of detail as there is so much going on. At the start of the extract a questioning sequence has been well under way when moderator Yvonne asks a non-elaborate follow-up question. There is a couple of seconds delay while Yvonne scans the group before Brian offers an answer – 'it's a nice van'. Before Yvonne can respond Dave has made a joke that a number of the members laugh at. The moderator ignores this and repeats Brian's answer 'yeah, it's a nice van'.

She then repeats something that another participant, Diana, had said in response to a previous question: 'the less Postman Pat the better'. Indeed, she repeats this and part of her question twice as the first time she is competing with a lot of laughter resulting from Dave's joke. Diana who has already, just prior to this extract, said that she did not want her van to look like a Postman Pat van offers another children's book example: 'not to look like a Noddy car'. On prompting this is unpacked as not wanting to 'look ridiculous' and wanting the van to look 'more like a car'.

After a short pause, moderator Yvonne continues with another question that is similar to the previous one. However, this one offers a candidate format. In the previous chapter we noted that when interaction gets complicated or hard to control moderators can move to asking questions which require descriptive accounts. The interaction here has got hard to control (note the joking and laughing) and perhaps rather repetitive in Diana's case. Whatever the precise reason, here moderator Yvonne asks for 'words'. This results in a classic repeat receipt sequence where the participants offer one- or two-word descriptive accounts and the moderator repeats them.

There are some exquisite details to these sequences. For example, note the way here that moderator Yvonne selects new speakers by eye gaze or pointing. Note also the intonation on the repeats. The rising or continuing intonation marks them as not (necessarily) complete or sufficient. Contrast a classroom situation where the teacher repeats pupils' suggestions and marks the right answer by a completing intonation. In the focus group there is no right answer, although there may be the right *kind* of answer.

As we have noted before, questions asking for descriptions followed by sequences of repeat receipts are commonplaces of focus groups. In the previous chapter we noted their use in breaking up talking or conflict between participants, and establishing more direct control of the inter-action. In this chapter we can add a number of further features. Repeat receipts:

- signal the worthiness of an answer;
- serve as a model for future answers;
- function like questions in selecting new group members by gaze or pointing;

- show that the moderator is attentive to what participants are saying;
- provide a quick way of getting responses for a range of group members;
- provide easily accessible responses for the tape and easily summarized responses;
- may pick out the most appropriate word or phrase from a more complex answer;
- manage the moderator's problem of avoiding showing expertise on the product through only using the participants' words (rather than glossing or formulating in a way that shows dangerous extra understanding).
- using only the participants' words emphasizes their creativity and spontaneity.

Let us linger for a moment on one or two points from this list. We have emphasized the moderators' dilemma of generating spontaneous interaction but guiding the nature of that interaction. Repeat receipts manage this dilemma by providing a considerable degree of shaping – words are requested, then appropriate answers are modelled – but not offering candidate answers of their own. We have also emphasized the trouble that can arise if moderators are seen as experts on the topic, and repeat receipts guide interaction without displaying dangerous skilled knowledge of the topic.

Another feature of these sequences is that they are fast. Responses are one or two words – they do not require accounts and justifications. Speed is underlined by the moderator snapping her finger when asking for more contributions. A repeat receipt sequence is an extremely compact way of getting contributions from across the group.

Repeat receipts and projective questions

One of the types of question that has been popular in market research is *projective questions*. These are supposed to provide particularly *deep* output. They are underpinned by psychoanalytic theory that suggests that market researchers need to penetrate the surface consciousness of rational thinking and socialization to deeper desires and fears (Branthwaite and Lunn, 1985). Krueger gives a range of such questions in his useful manual on developing questions. For example, a projective question he offers is: 'Suppose that this agency was a restaurant. What sort of place would it be and what would it be like?' (1998: 75–6). Questions of this kind are taken to access less conscious or rational judgements through their metaphorical nature.

We are not entirely convinced by the psychoanalytic story that is used to justify questions of this kind. However, they do seem to be interesting, revealing and useful in focus groups. Our general interactional perspective, combined with our specific observations about repeat receipts help understand the mechanisms which make questions like these effective. In particular, repeat receipts provide a way of modelling what appropriate answers should look like.

In what follows we consider a projective question in a focus group where the participants are enjoying playing a 'game' of *brand as person*. They were asked to consider the different brands of a product on the table as people who went to a party, and to decide which groups might be formed over the course of the evening. That is, if each brand is a person who talks to whom, and what about. The brands have now been moved into a set of distinct groupings on the table in the centre. (Note the brands are pseudonymized as capital cities.)

M: Colin	And the, (.) the large pile there, where Rio, Cairo, New York, Washington, (.) Cape and so on are, [well what is their common, (.) theme?	
Angie	[(xxxxxxxxxxx)	
M: Colin	Sorry?	
Angie	They are talking about men and women there,	
M: Colin	((laughs))	
Jim	just <u>sma:ll</u> [talk] (xxxx) too,	
Angie	[Yes,]	
→ M: Colin	Small talk,	repeat receipt
Jim	About pubs and discos,=	
Sam	=Yes, exactly,=	
Jim	=what's going on there, yes,	
M: Colin	Hm <u>mm</u>,	
Maggie	Talk about, (.) <u>clubs</u>	
Clare	Yes,	
M: Colin	And=the, (.) the, (.) group, with er, .hh the <u>Lon</u>don in it,	
Sam	They are sitting in front of the fireplace,	laughter
Jack	Well, they are at a wine-tasting	laughter
→ M: Colin	At a wine-tasting	repeat receipt
Angie	Talking about a concert,	
Jim	[Yes,]	
Sam	[where,] (.) they they were one night,	
→ M: Colin	Concert, (.) um mm,	repeat receipt
Jim	Yes, or also (with which [xxxxx)	
Sam	[Theatre, perhaps, (.) and art,	
Maggie	°Opening day, exactly,°	
→ M: Colin	<u>Opening day</u>, well,	repeat receipt

We will not go into much detail here. Suffice it to note again the way the repeat receipts pick out key descriptive terms, stripping off much of the contextual material. They model simple, brief answers. Note the way moderator Colin picks out terms that characterize or epitomize the social significance of the responses. For example, for the first brand grouping he repeats only 'small-talk', perhaps judging what comes after to be elaborations on this basic idea. When nothing new is forthcoming he moves on to the next group of brands. Note also the brevity of the participants' responses here. Even though the talk is lively, they keep to a few words. Indeed, the final offering from Maggie is the briefest, suggesting that the shaping role of repeat receipts has been effective.

Whether the moderator is able to shape the brevity of participants' contributions using repeat receipts or not, they remain as a highly visible guide in the interaction. The repeats stand as a record of what is important with the surroundings stripped. They also help prevent the interaction drifting off topic. Despite the animated talk here the moderator is easily able to move on to further questions.

Projective questions as requests for descriptive talk

One of the features of projective questions is that they typically require participants to produce descriptive accounts of some kind. They offer a candidate format that involves describing features of the world. In this, they contrast to questions that request POBAs. Asking for descriptive accounts can be a rather strange thing to do in everyday settings. Descriptive accounts are usually parts of practices where people are offering evaluations of some kind. The neat thing about the class of projective questions is that they provide a way of getting at descriptive accounts. One useful way of thinking about them is as questions which require people to invest psychological or social significance into descriptions.

In the previous example, the moderator's question contained a candidate format asking about the common theme of brands as people talking together. Note, this is not asking for opinions or views of the brands. Rather it is asking people to characterize the social significance of particular packaging.

We have noted above in a number of places that one of the things that moderators try to avoid is account clutter. Just as descriptive accounts are what we want, account clutter (expressions of doubt, caution, disclaimers and qualifications) is what we don't want. The risk in asking for descriptive accounts is that people's assertions about the world will be swamped in distracting clutter. This is most likely to be a problem where people construe the task as one with a right or wrong answer. One of the powerful characteristics of projective questions is that they generate an *as-if* world where there is no simple right or wrong. Product packets do not actually go to gallery openings together or make small talk. Projective questions, then, become a technique for avoiding account clutter.

Many of the features that are characteristic of moderators' practice of repeat receipts are found in a refined way in their use of the *whiteboard technique*. This is a common practice, and it adds something distinctive, so it is worth dwelling on it for a moment.

The whiteboard technique

Near the start of focus groups moderators often collect contributions of some kind and write them onto a flip-chart or whiteboard. As an exercise it has the virtue that it gets everyone involved at an early stage – many of the latter phases of the group allow much more differential responding. However, it has some more specific virtues that we wish to highlight.

Let us consider this with an example. The following is from a focus group concerned with shampoo adverts. At the start of the group the participants have been shown a video of a shampoo advert.

```
M: Martha    Just tell me em. what sorts of things came
             to mind not necessarily what you wrote
             down. But what sorts of things came to
             mind when I showed you that film just
             literally the first sort of thoughts
```

In what follows this extract, the participants offer a variety of ideas and thoughts, some quite complex, some simple. However, after each contribution, moderator Martha writes down just a word or two on her flip-chart. What she does is the equivalent of a repeat receipt. Having asked for descriptions (note – she has not asked participants' *opinions* of the advert, or whether they *liked* it) she strips off everything except key words. At this early stage in the group the whiteboard exercise provides a lesson in *focused* talk. The interactional pattern is the same as for repeat receipts:

Moderator	Asks for description	**directly or indirectly**
Member 1	Provides description	**a few words or a phrase**
Moderator	Writes down key word or words	**then orients to next member**
Member 2	Provides further description	
Moderator	Writes down description	**and so on . . .**

Correction and repair

Earlier in the chapter we noted that when moderators attempt to generate useful opinions they can do so before or after contributions from participants. They can shape the future or repair the past. Up to now we have noted the way candidate formats and candidate answers work to shape the way participants respond. In a sense, repeat receipts work both ways. On the one hand, they pick out and emphasize what is useful about a prior contribution. On the other, they provide a model to shape future responses. In this final section of the chapter we will concentrate on ways that moderators attempt to recast or modify participants' contributions. In studies of discourse and interaction this comes under the general topic of correction and repair.

Repair in everyday talk

Correcting another speaker in an everyday conversation can be a very delicate matter. Conversations are full of potential for slips and confusions – people pronounce names wrong, they mix up times and places, they make assumptions that are incorrect. This is not surprising given how complex the world is and how much we need to keep in mind in our dealings with other people. However, even when an error has been made (or has been judged to be made!) speakers are very cautious about correcting one another.

What happens more commonly in everyday situations is that the recipient will indicate that there has been a problem, perhaps by repeating the problem item, but not correct it. That is, they *initiate* the repair, but the first speaker, the person who made the mistake, does the actual *correction*. That is, the speaker will repeat the item correctly that has been indirectly indicated as a problem by the recipient. Sounds complicated! But the idea is simple enough in practice – the following example illustrates it:

```
        Speaker A   Hey (.) the first ti:me they stopped me
                    from selling cigarettes was this morning.
                    (1.0)
  →     Speaker B   From selling cigarettes?
        Speaker A   Or buying cigarettes.
        (from Hutchby and Wooffitt, 1998: 29)
```

Note the way here that speaker B initiates repair by repeating some of what speaker A said, with an emphasis on the mistaken word. But does so with a questioning intonation. This leaves it to speaker A, who made the mistake, to give the correct version.

The repair is thus *embedded* in the interaction rather than made explicit. And as such there is less of a requirement for the sorts of apologies, accounts and explanations that might follow an *explicit* rather than *embedded* correction. Conversation analysts talk of an interactional *preference for self-repair* that is sustained by these practices. This might sound a rather tortuous way of talking about something rather simple, but repair is a basic practice of interaction. These distinctions highlight common but fundamental practices involving repair. And repair is so important, and so delicate, because it involves a situation where one speaker may be questioning another's morality or competence.

Correction in focus groups

The sort of repair and correction that has been studied by conversation analysts involves specific words or items, and is typically done in situations where both parties to the conversation recognize the problem, at least after it has been pointed out. In focus groups, the sorts of situation we are interested in are rather more diffuse. What is at issue will often not be just individual words or items, but *types* of contribution – a style of answer, an unhelpful digression, an anecdote or an attempt to be a market research expert. Moreover, the problem may not be recognized by the group member. People are learning how to be good focus group participants on the job. This is part of what makes the task of moderation such a challenge – it almost always involves getting skilled actions out of novices!

Despite these differences, the general point about repair and correction holds. Correcting what people are doing and getting them to do something else instead is, potentially, a highly delicate task. It is not a task best done explicitly and publicly. Even while they are learning, people tend not to like being told that they are doing the wrong thing. It also goes against one of the other main tasks of the moderator that is to generate smooth interaction with contributions from the various participants. The trick is to keep people feeling that they are performing well, doing the right thing, and can say whatever comes to mind, but that being precisely what the focus group requires.

For these reasons corrections in focus groups tend to be indirect and inexplicit. Indeed, the trouble with studying correction in focus groups is that they are so inexplicit that they are not always easy to recognize *as* corrections. When studying groups we have drawn on our expertise in the practice in focus group moderation to identify practical techniques that moderators use to head off, stop, or rework things that participants are doing. We will focus on two techniques of correction:

- strategic use of continuers;
- asking new participants or questions.

In conversation *mm* can be used in a range of different ways. It can be used to acknowledge what has just been said, to encourage a speaker to continue, to raise a problem with what has just been said, or to make a (weak) evaluation. The most common use is as a piece of speech that acknowledges the preceding talk (technically an 'acknowledgement token'). Such a use is arrowed in the following extract:

```
        Mar     °M:m°, .hh b'd I've deferred panic fer the
                la:st two days, I keep- (.) th:inking about-
                .hhh life en dea:th, =an' people losing jo:bs,
                e[n:   ]
        Mal      [Ye:s]
        Mar     .hh en then conf'rence papers, =en panic see:m
                very mi:ld.
        Mal     ↑Mmmhhhh.
                (0.4)
        Mal     I: kno:w.
→       Mar     °Mm.°
                .hh Now listen, =ebout- temorro:w The Astor
                starts et . . .
                (Gardner, 1997: 134; slightly simplified)
```

Here we can see how the mm with the falling intonation (note the full stop after it) conveys that the speaker has nothing more to add to the topic and paves the way for a new topic.

Mms with a rising and then falling contour are used to express heightened involvement. They are often weaker alternatives to evaluative terms such as 'wow amazing'. In the following, Ron comments to Sally on an exciting music lesson their son had experienced.

```
        Ron     ↑(So:='t w')↓qui:(.)te- exc↑iting fer
                Don:,=rea:lly,
→       Sal     ↑Mm:.
                (1.0)
        Ron     ↑°Mm. (0.2) 't's good°↑
                (0.9)
→       Sal     ↓°He wz v↑ery plea::sed°↓
                (from Gardner, 1997: 147; slightly simplified)
```

Ron and Sally are displaying commitment in matters affecting their children, and the mm with intonation like this, the 'punched up' receipt, is a way of doing that.

The neat thing about mm interactionally is it has almost no propositional content (which makes it very flexible) and it allows different intonation to be displayed clearly. It is almost like a neutral passenger for intonation. This is seen most clearly in gustatory mms, as Sally Wiggins has shown. In the following Sandra and Ian have started to eat Christmas dinner; their pleasure is not hard to see:

Conversation Box 5.1   continued
Mmm

```
Sandra     ↑mmm (0.4) ↑mm↓mm↑m::
Ian        ↑mm↓m[m↑mmm:::m↑mmmm:
Sandra     ↑mmmm↓mmm:::
           (from Wiggins, 2002)
```

Want to know more?

Gardner's (2001) book is technical but full of wonderful observations about mms and similar parts of interaction. Wiggins (2002) links mms to eating and evaluation in a beautiful way.

Strategic use of continuers

One of the things that recent work in conversation analysis has shown is the importance of the little words and noises that traditional linguists did not have much time for. The sound 'mm' is a case in point. It is not really a word, but it can be invested with significance depending on context and intonation. Indeed, Rod Gardner (2001) has written a whole book about mm! It is very easy to produce mm with different sorts of intonational contour that mark out different uses. For example, flat intonation can make mm a 'neutral continuer', downward intonation can make it an 'acknowledgement token', and upward intonation can mark trouble and, possibly, initiate repair of that trouble.

Some studies have considered the use of mm in professional or work settings. For example, medical students, may be encouraged to provide frequent support for patients when they are reporting their problems by making mm-like sounds. However, Paul ten Have (1999) cautions that mm should be used sensitively and not too frequently. Indeed, he suggests that there are no simple recipes or rules and this makes it hard to train people in how to use mms effectively.

This point could apply equally to focus group moderation and the use of mms. It is hard to give simple recipes, and it would be hard to train people if they were not already competent everyday speakers. Nevertheless, we can note one use of mms in moderator correction and suggest that it is a practice that could be used and, cautiously, explored.

Let us start this exploration with an example to help us. This sequence is from an exercise where participants report on adverts they remember.

```
        Charles    (xxxxxxxxxx) >you're just looking at< this
                   price of this Po:lo
                   (0.4)
        Nik        Seems a very good advertising agency.
→   M: Zoe         hm mm, (.) hm mm,
        Bob        nah: I think definitely the best (0.2)
                   that, (0.2) the piano down↑stairs, (0.2)
                   >its like<
                   (0.4)
                   (xxx)
        Tim        °I know°=
        Bob        =like even the one with the (.) the piano      laughs
                   (more often it'll be now but it was at the
                   time
```

We have already noted that focus groups are not intended to collect together marketing experts to judge the quality of advertising agencies. They are done *for* marketing experts. Their role is to discover the *naïve* consumers' *genuine feelings* towards adverts. In this light we can see what Nik does in judging the advertising agency is not what is required of a focus group participant. However, this leaves moderator Zoe with a tricky dilemma. She can ask Nik to avoid this topic, or make some general statement about what focus groups are about. But, either explicitly or implicitly, this is likely to be heard by Nik as critical. And it may discourage him and others from taking part so spontaneously. She can just leave Nik be. But if she does this she may end up with more diverting discussion of advertising agencies.

What she does is something delicate and fascinating. She responds to Nik's turn with 'hm mm, (.) hm mm,'. It is very hard to convey the precise intonational quality of this pair of hm mm's. However, it injects just enough rising intonation to mix a receipt of what Nik has said with a sense that it is not quite right and encourage someone else to respond. The second hm mm with more stress on the mm is probably part of what selects a new speaker. Note also what the moderator Zoe does *not* do. She does not do a repeat receipt; she does not repeat 'good agency', say, directly afterwards to show that she has registered the importance and appropriateness of the turn before moving on to someone else. The absence of the standard repeat receipt combines with the delivery of the hm mm to move things on.

We are struggling slightly to make explicit something that works so indirectly – perhaps we need Rob Gardner to come and sort us out! But, whatever the precise mechanism, the upshot is clear. The topic of abstract judgements of advertising agencies is abandoned and when the contributors continue speaking they do so as naïve consumers. It might be a bit strong to characterize it so explicitly, but they take it as something like: 'Just carry on. Don't waste too much time playing experts!'

As an intervention this could hardly be more minimal. Nudging participants like this with little pushes in the *right* direction is pretty much the opposite of the long and elaborate question-constructions we met previously. But both have their roles in the moderator's delicate choreography of group process. In this case the minimal, oblique nature of the intervention is just what is required to avoid something that might be construed as critical or even telling the group member off.

Asking new participants or new questions

Moderators nudge the participants with little pushes in the *right* direction. Participants can easily be nudged in this way because they monitor the moderator very closely. Little indirect indications can have a powerful effect on the course of the interaction. This general attentiveness on the part of the participants has to do with what John Heritage (1997) has called the *asymmetry of interactional and institutional knowhow*. This asymmetry is expressed in two ways. First there is a very different involvement for the professional and client. For your doctor, say, your visit is part of her general routine of cases and diagnoses. For you, though, this is *your* unique problem that *you* require special and personal help with. Second there is different knowledge of protocol. Your doctor has several years of training and many previous consultations so is likely to be very familiar with a specific set of protocols which have their own reasons and histories. Without that training and experience you may find it much harder to predict how things will develop and what you should do. So you pay close attention to the professional to pick up cues and nudges about what you should do. Put another way, the goals of a professional or institutional arena such as a focus group may be quite *opaque* to the lay participants.

This opacity is heightened by the indications that something *specific* is being aimed at. When you turn up at a focus group it is not like your everyday life – you are paid to be there, to sit with a set of people you do not know, guided by a moderator, watched by video and one-way mirror, to do something valuable enough to be funded by a company, organization or political party, to have conversations about things in a way that is sometimes similar and sometimes very different from what you have done before. In his discussion of AIDS counselling, Anssi Peräkylä (1995) suggests that the opacity of the general frame of activity makes some kinds of action more attractive than others. In particular, group members are more likely to confine themselves to responsive actions rather than initiating actions. This makes sense – if you are unsure you follow the lead of others.

In focus groups, participants seldom ask questions, and are quick to follow the moderator when she or he asks things. When the moderator asks the ubiquitous 'what else?' it is immediately understood that the moderator would like to hear *more* and from *other* participants. This very simple, very basic, feature of moderators' questions can be exploited to deal with trouble or unwanted contributions. Not only is it a good way of generating new material it is an effective way of terminating what has been happening. For example, 'what else' can be used to generate new material; but it also appears where moderators are noticeably unconvinced or unimpressed by a specific answer or a whole line of discussion. It becomes a discrete form of repair.

Let us look at the following extract, in which the participants are given the task of describing an advertising film.

```
      M: Fiona   ↑How would you describe it- what words
                 would you use to descri:be it
                 ((23 turns omitted))
      Ally       Dull colours
                 (0.4)
  →   M: Fiona   >Yeh<                              does not look
                 (0.6)                              at Ally,
                 what else: (.)                     drinks, scans
                 other-other ways to describe it    group
                 (1.0)
      Bella      I li- I li:ke the: ↓uhm (0.2) image of the   M: Fiona looks
                 (0.2) >pregnant woman< and the (0.2) baby    at Bella
```

In some ways Ally's contribution 'dull colours' appears focus group appropriate. It is a brief description of the sort that we saw encouraged above in our discussion of repeat receipts. However, the contributions from others have focused on features of the people and their relationships. Whatever its merits to us, it is interesting to see how the moderator responds to it. The quick and shortened 'yeh' is notably less encouraging than other receipts given by the moderator. Also, she does not repeat 'dull colours' as she has the option of doing to display her appreciative recipiency and the appropriateness of the response. Indeed, she does not look at Ally, rather she leans forward to take a drink from a can of soda and then starts to scan the group as she asks 'what else'. In acting like this, moderator Fiona does not *explicitly* criticize Ally's contribution remark, but she does show her interest in other responses. Bella may well orient to this as she emphasizes aspects of the people in the advert and their image.

Here is another example to illustrate the way asking new questions can be a way of moving out of less useful stretches of interaction. The moderator has shown the group a series of vacuum cleaners and starts to ask the group about them. She has tried to get quick answers ('what comes immediately to mind?') and answers which relate to the image of the cleaners ('what image has it got?'). However, the participants have come out with a very lively and engaged set of responses, including a range of anecdotes about using particular cleaners, technical issues about design and power, as well as comments about image ('old fashioned'). The participants are frequently addressing each other during this discussion. This may be rich material for the marketing and design department, but it is complicated, and mixes different concerns together. It will be hard to report on as well as not being easy to assimilate from behind the one-way mirror. It is a bit like being served an excellent meal, but with all the courses turning up at the same time. After allowing this to continue for a while the moderator breaks in with a typical elaborate, projective question.

```
         Sarah       is that a water one as well?
         Jackie      cos don't they do a, (0.2) >a< double one
                     >sort of thing< for washing.
→  M: Amanda          Okay, (.) em,                        walks back to
                     .(0.2)                               chair
                     >can you,< (.) guess=
                     lets play a ga:me. (0.2)             picks up notes
                     Let's, (.) <imagine> that, e::m, (0.2)  touches cleaner
                     this one >(brandname)<
                     (1.0) comes to life. (0.4)
                     This is a person.
                     (0.2)
         Deirdre     hm mm,=
         M: Amanda   =walking through the door now. (0.2) What
                     type of person (>can you see<)? (0.6)
                     Right.=[what is this]
         Sarah            [   lady      ] in a <business suit>
```

Moderator Amanda comes in cautiously. Note the number of pauses and 'ems' after she has signalled a change with 'okay'. She builds to the projective exercise. This involves the group considering the set of vacuum cleaners again, but this time the projective element focuses the participants on issues of image and abstract design. This way of doing things eliminates both the anecdotes and the practical design comments. Sarah is the first of a number of participants who provides answers of the required kind.

By asking the new question moderator Amanda does three things. First, she terminates an overcomplicated and confusing piece of interaction that is only partly relevant to her concerns. Second, and less explicitly, she signals that a certain kind of responding is not helpful. Third, she instigates responding that is more relevant to her concerns.

Conversation Box 5.2
Explicit versus embedded repair

Repair – correcting another speaker – is one of the most delicate things you can do in conversation. When someone corrects the person they are speaking to this often leads to an account of some kind (an explanation or apology, or both). This can disrupt the flow of interaction. Here is an explicit repair where Mr O corrects the speaker on the desk ('I thought it was earlier than that').

	Desk	. . . but it's at- on three o'clock and she might just be free or between interviews. (1.0)
	Mr. O.	w-What time is it now sir?
1	Desk	Three isn't it?
2	Mr. O.	(We:ll?) I thought it was earlier than tha:t. (0.3)
3	Desk	It's two o'clock I'm sorry
	Mr. O.	Yeah.
	Desk	I got the hour wrong. But it's just two. Hfhh Okay let me call her and you call her in about fifteen or twenty minutes. (from Jefferson, 1987: 96)

This is a three-turn repair sequence – it starts with the mistake (1), the second speaker explicitly raises a problem (2), and the first speaker gives a new version correcting the mistake (3). Note in particular the way the Desk apologizes for the mistake and gives a (rather undeveloped!) account for it.

It is not surprising that ways of doing repair have evolved that manage this kind of problem. The most prevalent is to embed the repair in interaction without making the repair explicit. The following exchange takes place in a hardware store – the customer is trying to match the fitting on a pipe.

→	Customer	Mm, the wales are wider apart than that.
→	Salesman	Okay, let me see if I can find one with wider threads ((looks through stock))
	Salesman	How's this.
→	Customer	Nope, the threads are even wider than that. (from Jefferson, 1987: 93)

Note, how the Salesman, the expert, simply substitutes *threads* for *wales*, and how the Customer subsequently adopts the suggested usage. Here *correction* is being effectively achieved without the three-turn repair sequence we saw in the previous example. Furthermore, this *embedded* correction does not become an interactional issue – it does not lead to the provision of an account.

Correction by experienced focus group moderators is almost always embedded or indirect. Explicit correction is unlikely to facilitate relaxed and eager participants.

Want to know more?

Jefferson (1987) is the classic paper on conversational repair. It makes most of the key points in a very clear manner.

To sum up, then, moderators only need minimal pushes to guide the participants. Participants are closely attentive to what moderators are doing and their cues as to what is required and what is not. By asking other participants questions, or asking new questions, moderators can:

- terminate problem interaction;
- indirectly suggest that interaction is problematic;
- generate more suitable interaction.

SUMMARY

Focus group moderators have to manage a basic dilemma between allowing participants to speak freely and spontaneously and guiding them to say the right kind of things in the right ways in the right times. In this chapter we have suggested a number ways in which moderators can manage this dilemma.

Openings provide the first management opportunity. Moderators typically combine a stress on the openness, freedom and spontaneity of what is required from focus group participants with a range of guides to what specifically is required. One of the ways of doing this is to emphasize what being in a focus group will *not* be like (an interrogation, a test, school, a discussion of private matters), but noting that they *just, simply,* grant the opportunity to offer certain things (opinions, feelings, simple honest observations).

A further place for managing this dilemma is when asking questions. Questions are often constructed in an elaborate form. This is because they are doing a number of things at once. One of the ways in which questions can nudge answers in the required direction (towards POBAs, say, or brief descriptive accounts) is to provide candidate formats or candidate answers.

- Candidate formats guide the *format* of the answers that are required – emotions, say.
- Candidate answers guide the type of answer by providing examples of potential answers – these might be glosses ('you get annoyed') or reported speech ('what total rubbish').

Candidate answers are delivered in a way that prevents them being heard as a complete list of multiple-choice options. This is often done through intonation, incomplete items and hesitancy.

A major technique for guiding responding is to ask questions that require descriptions, and then to use repeat receipts after the answers. These involve the moderator repeating one or two words from the answer. These have a number of roles. Most importantly they:

- show that the moderator is attending and treating the answer as a worthy one;
- function as questions through selecting new group members by gaze or pointing;
- pick out the relevant word or phrase from a more complex answer, highlighting it for the tape or viewers;
- serve as a model for future answers.

Repeat receipts are also a way of managing the tension for the moderator in being a focus group expert, but not an expert on either the product or the participants' own psychology. Repeat receipts use only the participants' own words and in this way avoid glossing or formulating what they are saying, which might show that they have relevant product expertise.

Projective questions are a more specialized technique of eliciting descriptions. Their beauty is that they require descriptive accounts rather than POBAs, yet their metaphorical nature means that they are not subject to normal truth or knowledge tests. This heads off account clutter, discourages 'don't know' responses, and makes it less likely that participants will ask the moderator or expect the moderator to know the answer. Projective questions typically set up sequences of repeat receipts as the moderator guides and picks out relevant descriptions.

The whiteboard technique is a specialized tool for use with questions requiring descriptions. It becomes a particularly explicit and enduring way of showing what is important and guiding future responding.

The final section of the chapter considered the issue of repair and correction. Two techniques of correction were highlighted.

- The first involved strategic use of continuers. This involved the use of mms and mm hms, with appropriate timing and intonation, to indirectly suggest that an answer was inadequate and nudge participants to different kinds of answers.
- The second involved asking new participants or asking new questions. Again these could be used to suggest an answer was inadequate and nudge participants to a different kind of answer.

TURNING PRACTICES INTO STRATEGIES

STRATEGY ONE

Your task in the introduction to the group is to stress the openness of what will happen while providing a range of indirect suggestions about what will be required (e.g. talk about feelings and views). This will not be sufficient by itself, but it will start things off in the right direction.

STRATEGY TWO

One of the roles of elaborate questions is to provide guidance about the type of answer that is required, while at all costs avoiding turning the questions into exam questions. Use candidate formats and candidate answers to suggest what is appropriate. Make sure that the candidates do not seem like an exhaustive list of options but just a suggestive indication.

STRATEGY THREE

Ask questions that can be answered with descriptions. Use repeat receipts to model appropriate answers working round the group members who are offering answers. Use projective questions if you want to head off members' worries about getting their answers wrong. Early in the group use a whiteboard exercise to clearly establish appropriate types of answering.

STRATEGY FOUR

If participants start to get away from what is needed (e.g. they start to tell anecdotes, play marketing experts, play market research experts, question the moderator) use an indirect technique to nudge them in the right direction.

An mm or even a laugh may be sufficient if used in the right way. Perhaps you are not sure of the right way? Watch your own videos and monitor your uses of mms. You may find that some people are good at this and some simply are not.

The simpler approach is to use questions to break things up. Ask a new person the same question. Or ask a new question. Of course, you will need to have a range of alternative versions of the same question if you want to stay focused.

6 Producing Varied Opinions

Why do you run a focus group rather than interviewing an individual? One answer is that a group allows you to access a variety of different opinions. Variety is fascinating – sometimes it is just what you want. But it is also troublesome. It is practical trouble in keeping the interaction going smoothly; and it is analytic trouble in the problems it raises for how to record and interpret it. Diversity of this kind is both a good thing and a problem. It is something that you want, but it can be tricky to deal with. We need to know how a sufficient variety of opinions can be elicited. And we also need to know how to manage the problems that arise when different people offer different opinions. How is conflict avoided and the talk fashioned so it is suitable for the report, the video and the watchers? This chapter will be concerned with how the *range* of opinions and descriptions in a group is both produced and managed.

Writers about focus groups often place a premium on exploring and documenting a range of different opinions and responses. David Morgan and Richard Krueger (1993) suggest that a good introduction to a focus group will explicitly encourage the expression of disagreement. The rationale for this can be seen in the special form of generalizability that is sometimes claimed for focus groups. While public opinion polls try to generalize the strength of opinion in a poll to the general population, the focus group will be used to generalise the relevant set of concepts and dimensions from group to population. Edward McQuarrie and Shelby McIntyre call this 'domain of response type of generalization' (1987: 59). Likewise, Trudi Bers argues that focus groups are 'best used to identify attitudinal dimensions and not to quantify the extent to which these are held in any population or subgroup' (1987: 19).

Let us consider this in terms of an example. A public opinion poll on the future of private health care might be attempting to assess the strength of support for increased private health insurance, private involvement in state hospitals and so on. It might end up with figures – for example, 43 per cent of people support the increased use of private health insurance. However, a focus group on private health care might identify a range of relevant things. These might include images of private health care as clean and wait free, or images of selfish and corrupt politicians supporting private care. It might identify concerns – 'Will I be unable to afford a hip replacement when I am old?' 'Will joining a private health scheme mean that I am seen as selfish?' 'Is public health "old-fashioned", "friendly" or whatever?'. The point of our (perhaps rather clumsy) made-up example is that the focus group will be unlikely to arrive at a percentage in support of a social policy like this. However, it might be able to do something at least as important, which is to identify the issues, worries, dimensions and images through which that policy is understood. If you are a politician developing a policy of publicly funded health provision these might be the things that help you the most. This is what focus groups researchers mean when they argue, as Mary Brotherson (1994) does, that focus groups are designed to elicit the *diversity* and *variety* in the data.

It might sound from this that conflict and diversity are what is required of a good focus group. Conflict will throw up the full range of images and evaluative dimensions; and you will want as much diversity as you can from your participants. However, this is too simple a view. Too much conflict will make the group unmanageable and chaotic. It will be hard work to run. And it will be equally hard work to report on. The clients will struggle to follow what is going on behind the mirror and on the tape. It may seem boring, but what is required is a *middle way*. Good moderation needs to be able to generate a spread of different themes and opinions without things becoming submerged in argument.

There are also focus group tasks for which too much diversity will be straightforwardly unhelpful. Consider a situation where Product Management has developed a line extender to an existing brand with modified packaging. They liaise with the advertising agency and market researchers to get a first general impression of its acceptability to the target group. Once the advertising people and product managers are installed behind the one-way mirror to watch the group they are not going to be helped by even a coherent mass of diversity. Some more general, or even consensual responses may be more helpful.

The issue of diversity, then, will partly depend on what the group is being run *for*. However, we hope to suggest some ways in which moderators can effectively manage issues of agreement and disagreement, consensus and argument. We will note the way moderators can draw on everyday interactional skills to elicit variety without it becoming chaotic diversity. Let's start with a way of thinking about beliefs and consensus that will be helpful to us.

A mundane world and variable views

The sociologist and ethnomethodologist Melvyn Pollner (1987) argues that most of the time people work with a fundamental assumption that there is a unitary world where everyone in the same position will see it in the same way. When we discuss things that happened, who did what and where, we assume we all have access to the same underlying reality. He calls this *mundane reason*. This is a basic working assumption that we use for understanding our world. For this reason we expect consensus or agreement over such things, and look for reasons if it breaks down.

One of the ways of understanding POBA talk is in contrast to this – it is as a world of potential variety, of *multisubjectivity*. When people describe views, opinions, attitudes and so on they are describing something that can be different. As Michael Billig puts it:

> The discourse of views, far from being based upon competing claims about external reality, will be based on statements describing different subjectivities. (1991: 171)

The point about talk of opinions and attitudes is that variation is *built into* the notions. In contrast, talk of facts should be unitary. Thus, if two people give us directions to a restaurant and each says it is on a different street we will want to resolve the contradiction. Who has got it wrong? Are they thinking of different eating-places? It is most likely that the restaurant will be on a single street. However, if these two people give us different reports on how much they *enjoyed* their goat's cheese tartlet we will not necessarily expect to arrive at some consensus. There is no mundane reason at work here driving us to think that only one is right. People can have different opinions of goat's cheese tartlets, different views; indeed, if they all had precisely the same view that might be the odd thing.

This shows again the interactional value of POBA talk for the task of moderating a focus group. POBA talk is precisely the kind of talk where diversity is appropriate. It need not be resolved. POBA talk is, potentially, talk that can provide diversity without conflict. One participant has this view; another participant has a different view. The down side of this POBA talk is that the interactional organization of assessments means that once one participant has offered an opinion or attitude it then becomes something for other participants to orient to. The more clearly this POBA item is an assessment then the more the preference for agreement will kick in and lead the next speaker to produce a similar assessment. We noted in the previous chapter how questions that attempt to get directly at descriptive accounts can head off this cycle of agreements. This means that these questions can also be effective for generating diversity. They head off the tendency to agreement with assessments. There are tricky issues here. Let us consider how they are actually managed by moderators, starting with, well, starting.

Diversity and group openings

It is helpful to think of the moderator managing a number of delicate problems in the course of the group. She or he needs to encourage participants to use POBA talk because this is talk that supports multi-subjectivity and therefore diversity. She or he also needs to manage two dangers. On the one hand, there is the danger that this diversity will result in vigorous conflict and argument that will obscure the issues. On the other, there is the danger that following the general preference for agreement with assessments, the talk will simply follow any kind of evaluative tendency that opens the topic.

These tensions between the tendencies towards conflict and towards consensus can be supplemented with a further set of issues. There is a concern that the moderator will be seen as having an investment in the product or being a representative of the policy being discussed. So another issue to manage is potential for participants to produce positive assessments whatever they think.

We will show how these concerns are picked up in some group introductions. Controversy and consensus are delicately handled. Moderators depict themselves as collecting contributions of different kinds that are offered in a simple, freestanding way (e.g. 'chipped in').

The following sequence is taken from the very beginning of a group on mobile phones. This is quite a long sequence and this time we have decided to simplify it to highlight this theme. We have taken out some digressions and displays of informality and left the segments that highlight particularly the issue of variation and conflict.

1	→ M: Lucy	Those who haven't been to a- a discussion group before the idea is getting a number of people to get to get many different ideas.	variation
2	→	So we are certainly not looking for consensus.	not consensus
3	→	Your friends talk about mobile phones I think, isnt it, which shouldn't be too controversial I think.	not controversial
4	→	Just chip in your ideas.	chip in ideas
5	→	Yknow people don't do research just to hear nice things certainly about new ideas .hh they are really looking for guidance.	not want nice things
6	→	So if you do end up making criticism don't feel that you have been unhelpful. It may be just as instructive as any nice things.	don't avoid bad things

Note the way that moderator Lucy starts off, early in her introduction, emphasizing the importance of getting different ideas. Placing this point at the start underlines its significance. At point 2 we see Lucy develop the idea of different ideas as contrary to consensus. So she is heading off any expectation that people might have that the group is meant to come to a joint position. However, at point 3 we can see this focus on difference and avoidance of consensus softened a bit. It should not be 'too controversial'. Thus the expectation is not of a major dispute.

This is backed at point 4 by a practical suggestion. Participants are encouraged to 'just chip in' their ideas. 'Chip in' is a lovely metaphor – the idea is, presumably, from golf where a chipped ball is hit up and onto the green from long grass or over an obstacle. The neat thing is that the chipped ball comes out of the air. In terms of the focus group discussion, it is not responding to, or commenting on, another's views. So this is a simple suggestion designed to head off participants commenting on each other's views or disagreeing with one another. Chipping in is a form of delivery of POBAs that cuts across the interactional patterns of assessments and second assessments, encouraging, agreement. It also cuts across the pattern of assessments and criticisms, discouraging argument.

Points 5 and 6 emphasize the value of being negative. That is, being negative is constructed as something that can be helpful and instructive. It is designed to divert any pressure that might be felt on the part of participants to be generally positive and supportive. In this example, then, we see the moderator attending to various concerns that relate to variation and the offering of different views.

Let us take another example to flesh this out a bit more. Again we are focusing on the way the moderator picks out a number of themes related to diversity and consensus, and their own stake in the product. And as before we will select the elements addressing these ideas to simplify what is going on in a rather complex introduction. We have again provided a much lighter transcription as we are concerned with the overall way in which the moderator organizes his introduction. The group is addressing advertising ideas in the area of IT.

```
1  →  M: Saul  Now we are starting late but the aim is to
               finish at nine thirty, which is when we
               promised. So I am going to keep- gallop
               through this. Which means I might have to      silencing will
               shut some of you up. Don't be offended         be due to time
               please. By that.                               pressure
2  →           It is important that I hear from               everyone
               everybody. I don't want any one individual     involved
               kind of dominating the discussion because      no individual
               yo- you are representing >you know<            dominating
```

hundreds of people so it is important to
get all the views here.

3 → And =em, (0.4) as- again as I mentioned   not after
it's ↑not there's not (0.2) a question of   consensus
getting a consensus view:. (0.2)

4 → You may (.) if you're the one person   contribute
sitting there thinking >I don't agree with   disagreements
the rest of them< plea:se >for goodness'
sake< speak up, cause, (0.6) eh (.) it's
important for me to have a- (.) all the   add alternative
different kind of perspectives (.)   views

5 → an- and if there's a kind of continuum of   tap continuum
opinion to get it ↓all.

6 → Let me just tell you who I am so that
you're clear. I work for a little known
company called Zappy Research. But we are
an independent market research company.
And that independent bit is the most
important thing about us. Because you'll
see: tonight that we are looking at some
advertising ideas. We didn't have
anything to do with these ideas.
We didn't create them.
I am not going to get upset if you hate   does neutrality
them. I'm not going to get a bonus if you   with respect to
love em.   object
So I am independent of the advertising
interests here.

7 → So frankly I am here to be as objective as   not need nice
it is possible. And I want you to bear   things
that in mind so. You don't have to say
nice things to keep me happy.

8 → As long as you explain why you have a   justify views
point of view that's all that matters.

9 → Clearly I can't go back to my clients and   justifies
say °I spoke to these eight people and   justification
they all thought all these ideas were
a:↑bsolute rubbish°. If I haven't got
some kind of justification that's it

This is quite a long sequence. However, there is a lot going on in it and it
serves as a good example of the range of business that can be done in
openings. Note also that people are settling in their sofas during the start of
the sequence. One of the participants opens a bottle of wine and pours for
some others. The delivery throughout is relaxed and friendly.

Note in point 1 that moderator Saul begins with an apology for starting
the group late. However, this is neatly turned round to a commitment to
finish on time, and therefore an account for possibly having to shut up

contributors. If he does that it will be in the group members' own best interests!

He then moves at point 2 to emphasizing that he wants contributions from across the group with no individual dominating. However, at point 3 he emphasizes that he is not after a consensus. And at point 4 he develops this idea by voicing what a group member might think and encouraging them to join in. Very neatly he encourages this by stressing how important it is to get 'all the different kind of perspectives', thus implying that this will be a topic where, at least potentially, there is a range of alternatives or, as he puts it in point 5, a 'continuum of opinion'.

Points 6 to 9 move on to a different concern. We have already considered part of this sequence in an introductory way in Chapter 2. Here we will develop that thinking. Moderator Saul manages his potential stake and interest in the discussion in a way that discursive psychologists have discussed (Edwards and Potter, 1992). Specifically he highlights his neutrality with respect to the advertising ideas. This is emphasized with a three-part list rather like that found in many political speeches before applause:

1 **We didn't ̲create them.**
2 **I am not going to get ̲upset if you hate em**
3 **and I am not going to get a bonus if you love em.**
   So I am independent of the advertising interests here

The upshot of the list is spelled out explicitly at the end – he is independent.

Interestingly in point 7 moderator Saul adds a further theme: the participants do not have to say nice things to keep him happy. However, this is tied to what will, implicitly, make him happy, which is 'explaining why' a point of view is held. In point 9 this is further tied to the demands that will be made of him by the clients.

In the next example we see moderator Phil emphasizing the likelihood of variations and encouraging the participants to deliver different views.

```
M: Phil      ((continues)) A::nd, (.) you might have a
             different view (xxxxxxxxx) across the, (.)
             em group. (.) And that's fine. (.) Eh I
             don't want you to sit there and think
             >'Oh I don't agree with, (.) what is being      active voicing
             said here.'<=I'd much rather that you, (.)
             tell what you think.
             ((lines omitted))
             It's it's gonna be a friendly, (.) e:m (.)
             open experience hopefully
             ((continues))
```

One of the things that moderator Phil does in the introduction above is actively voice the thoughts of participants. These voicings highlight positions that people might find themselves in and suggest actions. This is a common feature of moderator introductions when they are addressing issues of variation and consensus.

Let us just consider one final example to give an indication of how elaborate this can get. This is from a group concerned with body lotion (hence the reference to skins).

```
1  → M: Candy  You are all eight eh different
                individuals.
                probably with, (.)                         smiley voice
                different skins                             3 part listing
                different, (.) you know different, (.)
                habits
                different family situations                variation
                so lots of time and you don't have much
                time whatever, (.)
                and we all individuals in different em
                situations
2  →            so, (.) em if you're sitting there and
                somebody else says
                < 'O:h, (.) I do this' >
                and you think                               active voicing
                God how dreadful                            laughter
3  →            Plea:se (.) say that                        smiley voice
                it's really what we are here to hear.
                Yknow what everybody- everybody does
```

Here moderator Candy starts with an elaborately developed emphasis on difference between the group members. Then in point 2 she voices what a participant might be thinking in the face of what someone else has said ('God how dreadful'). In point 3 she strongly encourages members to contribute alternatives such as this. There is a detail here that is worth emphasizing. Although moderator Candy's active voicing is rather critical – 'God how dreadful' is a rather extreme criticism – its delivery is playful. Indeed, the extreme response to the use of body lotion might be one of the things that generates the laughter (as Derek Edwards, 2000, has shown, making a description sound extreme can be a way of making it ironic). This is rather neat. If we consider the aim is to generate variety without conflict, this is encouraging taking part, while keeping a light playful tone. It does not sound like a command to criticize one another.

Let us sum up. We suggest that moderators start to handle the tensions and issues that arise when generating a variety of views in their introductory comments. The following points are commonly made.

- *Variety*: Moderators emphasize that people have different views, perhaps because 'we are all different'. They request variety in their introductions.
- *Descriptive accounts*: Moderators emphasize their interest in POBA talk. However, they also stress the value of providing justifications for POBAs, and these justifications will be in the form of descriptive accounts.
- *Inhibitions*: Moderators encourage people to overcome any inhibitions on responding. This is often done by actively voicing thoughts that participants might have. This has two forms – (a) the acceptability of disagreeing with other participants is stressed; (b) the acceptability of being critical of the product is stressed.
- *Stake management*: Moderators stress their separation from the product. This emphasizes that they are not helped or made happy by positive comments.

In addition to these issues, moderators address the issue of conflict in a number of ways. Three of these are particularly important.

- *POBA talk*: One of the fundamental interactional virtues of POBA talk is that it is a discourse of multisubjectivity – it allows for different opinions or perceptions.
- *Downplaying conflict*: Moderators often present conflict as unlikely or rather trivial. They may present disagreements as unusual.
- *Chipping in*: Moderators construct the activities of participants adding their own views not as *disagreeing* but as *chipping in*. That is, they encourage the participants to provide their views in a freestanding way rather than to do so in contrast to the views of others. The focus group is presented as a collecting tank for varied POBAs.

Managing disagreement

In this section we consider some techniques that moderators can use to manage disagreement and prevent it undermining the success of the group. In effect the task is to generate variation in opinions without the various features of disagreement and conflict that arise in everyday situations. Moderators have a powerful position in groups as they are in a position to introduce new topics, shift topics, close down topics as well as select new speakers and close down current speakers. These activities are potentially delicate, and one of the skills in moderation is to manage them carefully and effectively. Our interest here is in how they are deployed to manage differences of opinion between participants.

Part of the power moderators have comes from the special turn organization in focus groups compared with everyday talk and some research

In interaction research neutrality is not considered a psychological attribute of a person, but something to be achieved and managed. Neutrality is something that comes up between friends – 'whose side are you on here' – and in institutional settings such as news interviews, relationship counselling and legal proceedings. It can be important in focus groups in two ways. The moderator needs to be neutral with respect to the product; and he or she needs to be neutral with respect to the different participants. Failures to display neutrality like this can impede the flow of the group and inhibit the participants from expressing certain views.

There are various ways of managing neutrality. One common approach in news interviews is to manage the *footing* from which you speak. Is your footing that of a person expressing your own views, or are you merely reporting someone else's? We are very attentive to these differences in talk, and careful to show when quoting other people or expressing our own views. Steve Clayman (1992) has shown that news interviewers typically shift footing when they are asking contentious questions. They do this by couching the contentious point in a quote from someone else. Here is a typical example:

```
Interviewer    You heard what Doctor Yalow said earlier in
               this broadcast she'll have an opportunity to
               express her own opinions again but she seems
               to feel that it is an EMinently soluble problem.
               and that ultimately that radioactive material
               can be reduced, to manageable quantities.
               'n put in thuh bottom of a salt mine.
Interviewee    Thuh p- thuh point that she was making earlier
               about (.) reprocessing of: thuh fuel rods goes
               right to thuh heart (.) of thuh way a lotta
               people look at this particular issue . . .
               (Clayman, 1992: 168)
```

Note the way the interviewer couches the strong critical point in terms of a quote from an earlier speaker. And note also the way the interviewee goes along with this – whether they think interviewers are against them or not, they typically treat them as not having their own views.

Want to know more?

For a summary of work on footing and neutrality see Potter (1996: 142–9). For a discussion of news interviews and interaction more broadly see Clayman and Heritage (2002).

discussion groups. As we have discussed elsewhere (Puchta and Potter, 2002), participants overwhelmingly address their contributions to the moderator rather than to each other. The moderator thus acts as a buffer, potentially softening conflict between individual's opinions. Even when the talk is building on, or critical of, another participant the moderator is more likely to be the person addressed.

Moderators tend to use one of two strategies when managing variability and discouraging its degeneration into conflict between participants. These two are:

- Quickly shift to a less 'dangerous' topic.
- Avoid explicitly formulating the disagreement.

When argument does break out things are tricky. It is not common, but we will address one example to show some of the things that could be done.

Shift to less 'dangerous' topics

We will start with an example that shows the way the moderator can shift topics to manage conflict. This extract is taken from a focus group on tyres. We cut to the interaction after the moderator has presented an advertising idea using a steering wheel rather than a tyre.

```
Rich         But that's not showing, you like to see,
             showing you the steering wheel is crazy.
             >It doesn't even show a picture of the car
             trade or anything does it<=
M: Gemma     =Well (.)ass- assuming we all know (.)
             °know the product°
Bill         A new driver=A NEW DRIver that looks at
             that doesn't know anything about tyre
             brands >won't know< what its about.
             (..)
M: Gemma     Okay, assum- assuming >that they< knew,
             (.) that it was tyres would, (.) that, (.)
             then be a barrier? (.) °or is there any
             other problem with that?°=
```

We will take this extract in two segments. In the first we can see moderator Gemma struggling with Rich and Bill's very strongly expressed views. We have already noted that in their opening speeches moderators may discourage members from expressing their views too strongly. Here we have an example of Rich offering a very strong view. This advert is 'crazy'. We can imagine that it leaves the rest of the group in a rather tricky position. Offering any alternative will be hard to do without it seeming to be in a major conflict with Rich. So it is not surprising that we see moderator Gemma coming in very fast. She develops the question to try and make the advert less crazy.

The problem for moderator Gemma is that Bill comes in with strong support for Rich's point. He is very emphatic in pressing the issue of new drivers coming to the advert – not putting aside people who do not know the product as moderator Gemma suggests. There is another problem with this from a focus group point of view: Bill is being a social theorist, generalizing about new drivers rather than reporting his expert knowledge of his own POBAs. Moderator Gemma again tries to reformulate the question. Note the slightly exasperated 'okay' and the further attempt to turn it into as 'as-if' question ('assuming') where *actual* drivers who do not know about tyres do not matter.

Moderator Gemma's attempt to deflect the line of argument is not successful. Rich again reiterates what 'you like to see' in an advert, returning to his unwelcome role as a social theorist. Other participants build on this as they report what they look for in a car advert. This is interesting and potentially relevant, but not what the moderator had asked. The moderator lets this carry on for a minute or two – perhaps because of its relevance, perhaps because she has already had two attempts to move the focus. Then this happens:

```
Rob          That looks upmarket there=I mean it
             doesn't tell me anything particular about
             the tyre, but, (.) its,=
M: Gemma     =What about the line 'the best ca:r'.
Basil        Doesn't do °anything° for me
```

What Rob does here is return to the advert. He gives a brief focus group style description (he has been well trained!), but then does something more troubling. He highlights the potential point of conflict. This is a dangerous moment. Will Rich and Bill start to dispute with Rob? Moderator Gemma heads it off. She comes in very quickly with a new question, moving the topic away from the image and onto the text.

The general point, then, is that variable opinions can lead to arguments, and moderators may ask a new question or use some other topic shift device to stop them developing. We also saw the way extreme views can cause problems that moderators try to head off.

Avoid explicit formulations of disagreement

In this section we will briefly consider another moderator strategy – which is to avoid explicit formulations of disagreement. Here we will consider a case where contrastive views are not formulated as such, and where the moderator avoids making the implicit contrast explicit.

The following extract is from a focus group concerned with features of cars. The participants are walking around a large space inspecting a number of different vehicles and being asked to comment on them.

Stuart	They've <u>all</u> got the curved window. (.) That I:: find it just a little bit, (.) yknow, >a bit< <u>too</u> big=
M: Walter	=What? this is (.) too much=
Stuart	=yeah,
M: Walter	Is too far extended. I think it may be just a little bit shorter. you've got a <u>lar</u>ge quarter light window here. (.)
Cliff	The the vision is superb (.)
Stuart	yeah, it is [superb]
Cliff	[(xxxx)]
Stuart	Without a doubt without a doubt. This °obviously is° larger compared with all the others.
Ginny	(xxxxxx)
Stuart	Yeah, [I]
Ginny	[(xxx)]
Stuart	I just- I just push the handle in to make the bonnet °(open)° (.)
Teddy	Are they trying to get away from the old ((Car Name)) stubbed nose bonnet by doing <u>tha</u>t ((clears throat)) Otherwise you're back aren't you.
M: Walter	Okay. (.) so these <u>fir</u>st did well for (.) e:h (.) the reason primarily >I guess< <u>si</u>ze. (.) A >little< more car like. Those who have been saying is a little more com<u>pact</u> (.) and, (.) got versatility in here, to be able to fold down your seats

Let us make a few simple observations about the way this unfolds. First note the contrast between Stuart's turn at the start of the extract where he describes the window as 'too big' and Cliff's assertion that 'the vision is superb'. Stuart has produced his criticism in a very tentative manner ('a little bit', 'you know'). Cliff's assertion is direct and unhedged, but addressed directly to moderator Walter, without any orientation to Stuart and potential disagreements.

This is the kind of interaction that moderators are after when they encourage participants to *chip in* their views. That is, variety is generated without it becoming diverted into argument. This is facilitated by the pattern of interaction, with talk being addressed to the moderator (who offers non-assessing receipts) rather than to one another. This is also facilitated by the softened way in which Stuart constructs his view. Indeed, he comes in after Cliff to *agree* with his point about vision. This might be a change of view, or highlighting a different facet of a big window (looks ugly, perhaps, but is good to see through). Moderator Walter might have followed this up – but it might have led to more distraction rather than clarification. There is only so much time for moderators to explore the detail of any one participant's claims.

Note the way that moderator Walter avoids this contentious issue in his summing up. He concentrates on themes where there has not been disagreement thus avoiding the need to explicitly formulate its nature.

Feature collecting for variety without disagreement

In the final section of this chapter we will consider one technique that moderators can use to generate variable opinions in a compact manner without strong disagreements. We have called this feature collecting for reasons that will become obvious (if they are not already obvious!). First, however, let us further consider the difference between market research and social science focus groups.

Social science focus groups

Greg Myers has done a number of important studies of the organization of talk in social sciences focus groups. He concludes that they are a:

> complex collaborative project operating under the shared assumption that the purpose of the discussion is to display opinions to the moderator. (1998: 85)

This emphasis on displaying opinions is similar to the stress we have seen in market research focus groups on the production of POBAs. Myers suggests that participants work hard to manage disagreements with one another to minimize conflict. Even where there are direct disagreements between participants it is often presented as an agreement with one aspect of a previous participant's turn. Nevertheless, in contrast to market research focus groups, the participants in social science groups are deliberately contentious. Myers writes:

> A frequent pattern, once discussions have gotten going, is that some of the more vocal participants present themselves as devils' advocates –

deliberately presenting their views as different from those of other participants, as an addition to what the group has presented so far (1998: 104).

Rather than obscuring variation, this pattern highlights it.

Myers illustrates this deliberate contentiousness with the following extract.

```
    M1       I would I would go with whoever said that=
    Mod.     =right - that's interesting because -
             Warwick you said you didn't agree? (1.0)
→   M2       no - I I'm being quiet - going to be
             deliberately contentious here - I think
             er, as much as we are all saying as much
             as it's nice to look at the environment
             and looking at concerns - we have a cozy
             middle class attitude here ((continues))
             (from Myers, 1998: 104)
```

What we see with M2's contribution is that instead of playing down disagreement, he highlights it. However, producing disagreement as a devil's advocate does presents it as something that is a contribution to the group. In a sense it highlights disagreement while downplaying its personal nature. After all, the devil's advocate is not actually the devil – devil's advocates are not meant to hold the views *themselves*, they *represent* them for the purposes of argument.

Feature collecting

The kind of contentiousness seen in social science focus groups is largely absent from market research focus groups, even in playful or devil's advocate form. While the devil's advocate heightens disagreement, albeit in a manageable way, market research moderators work to minimize disagreement and, when it does appear, tend to discourage participants following it up with each other. Instead, the main approach market research moderators use to collect varied opinions is to use a questioning technique we call *feature collecting mode*. One of the key aspects of feature collecting mode is that it is an attempt to cut across issues of agreement and disagreement by moving from assessments to the sorts of descriptive accounts that might warrant those assessments.

Feature collecting mode involves the encouragement of brief descriptive answers on a particular topic in a round robin manner. We have already seen examples of this in our discussion of repeat receipts where we considered the way good answers can be elicited, and the way anecdotes and personal narratives can be headed off. Here our interest is in the way *variety* can be generated without argument. At the same time we will highlight the way feature collecting tends to place some restrictions on the variety of opinions produced.

We will use two examples here, both from the same group concerned with vans. We have seen part of the first in the previous chapter.

```
→  M: Yvonne   What do you think=what sort of wo:rds       request for
              would you use to describe >if it was your<  description
              ide_al van. (.) yeah? (.) .hh and it was
              less, (.) less Noddy>like< if you like.
              (0.2)
              What sort of words would you use to         reiteration
              describe the ideal=
              what [would it look] like                   reiteration
   Graham            [Stylish        ]
→  M: Yvonne   Stylish,                                   repeat receipt
              (1.0)                                        moderator
                                                           gestures for
                                                           more

   Diana      Practical.
→  M: Yvonne   Practical,=what else.
              ((snaps her finger))
              (1.0) What would your ideal lo_ok like.      points at Keith
              (1.0)
              °(say about you (0.2) >and< your company)°
   Keith      A bit sporty?
   Steve      Sma:rt
→  M: Yvonne   A bit spor↑ty (0.2) ↑smart                 repeat receipt
              (1.0)                                        scans group

   M: Yvonne  Okay, what about number si_x. (0.2) Who
              chose number si_x.
```

Note the way that moderator Yvonne has requested *descriptive words* for the *ideal* van. So this is a *descriptive* rather than *evaluative* question, and it is *projective* rather than *judging*. That is, the participants are asked to give brief descriptions of an imaginary *ideal*, rather than making descriptive judgements of an *actual* van.

Using the standard receipt repeat technique the moderator gathers a range of descriptions. The ideal van would be: *stylish, practical, sporty* and *smart*. There is variety here, and even some contradiction – could a van be practical, stylish and sporty? Perhaps. We can imagine it as the by-line on a van advert: the new Dolloravan: stylish and sporty, yet completely practical. However, the style of asking about an *imaginary* van, and an *ideal* van, lessens the chance of interactional problems arising from participants producing variable descriptions. Participants can have their own special features of a van that makes it ideal. Feature collecting here is fairly straightforward.

Take the next example as a contrast. This is from later in the same group. The participants have been asked to consider some pictures of vans cut out and pasted on cards (this is prior to looking over some actual vans). We have already made comments on some other aspects of this extract in Chapter 3. As before moderator Yvonne starts with a descriptive question.

```
M: Yvonne     What ↑words would you use to describe this     descriptive
              van.                                           question
              (.8)
David         Su↑perb
              (2.0 - some participants laugh quietly)        moderator
                                                             smiles
M: Yvonne     ↑Yeah (.6) what else
David         Sporty. (.) trendy.
              (1.3)
M: Yvonne     What about the rest of you
              you're pulling faces.
              You're going. (.) you're shaking your
              h↓ead                                          some murmuring
              (1.4)                                          descriptive
              Tell me what words you use to describe         question
              this van
Alan          °can you can you say it's like sporty and
              trendy°
Graham        ((laughs))
Keith         I think it looks sexy.                         murmuring and
                                                             soft laughter
M: Yvonne     Cmon tell me what you really think. (.9)       murmuring
              Words >to< describe this car                   descriptive
              how would you describe it                      question
Malcolm       I just don't like. (.) er (.) the box
              °>(it [looks like a box)<°]
Mod.               [Yeah. you don't     ] like the box.      repeat
Yvonne        So how would you describe it.
                                                             descriptive
                                                             question
              (1.0)
Malcolm       °A van°
```

The difference between this extract and the last that we want to highlight is that the previous question asked people about their *ideal* van, and this asks about an *actual* van. This potentially generates two kinds of problem. First, when people are asked to imagine their own ideal – this can be a personal task; people may have different ideals (just like you do not have to have the same favourite food as other people). However, when they have an actual van differences in description or evaluation may be more accountable. Second, when people are asked about their ideal van this keeps everyone in the area of positive evaluations. However, in this case there is an actual van, so there may be a range of positive and negative assessments. The question in this extract, then, may cause difficulties if people offer different descriptions and different assessments. There may be more of a problem with just 'chipping in' without it seeming to be a disagreement with another speaker.

What we see in this example is a bit of trouble. After moderator Yvonne's question David comes in with a very strong evaluation, albeit offered with questioning intonation. The strength of this evaluation combined with the type of question may make it more difficult for others to offer responses that provide variety. Indeed, some other group members seem to suggest their disagreement indirectly with quiet laughter. And in response to the 'what else?' question the same participant elaborates on his answer with more positive descriptions: 'sporty, trendy'.

This is a tricky environment in which to offer contrastive descriptions. The moderator resorts to something unusual, which is to suggest that people have negative opinions because of their facial expressions. And, indeed, there is some indication that the next responses ('sporty', 'trendy', 'sexy') are treated as ironic. The laughter continues and moderator Yvonne asks them 'what they really think'. This finally generates a much more critical description – 'looks like a box' – which is incorporated into a new question that elicits a further description: 'a van'.

We have spent a bit of time on this example. The point we are illustrating with it is that even feature collecting can get into the same kinds of problem that evaluative questions generate. Participants can have trouble responding because of potential conflict between their different responses. Part of the problem is that there is no clear-cut distinction between descriptive and evaluative terms. Words like 'sporty' and 'trendy' are often seen as strongly evaluative, and can therefore generate the same issue of the management or agreement and disagreement as words like 'love' and 'poor'. However much moderators stress they should 'just chip in', that 'everyone has their own views' and that people should 'speak up if they disagree' it is not so easy to override general conversational practices in which people are reluctant to offer disagreeing second assessments. Moderator Yvonne has to work quite hard here to elicit varied responses.

Let us follow this issue through with one final example. This involves a classic projective question. The moderator asks participants to imagine the brand as a person, and describe his or her characteristics.

```
M: Brown    And the characteristics of this ↑pe:rson      projective
            (.) if you can imagine them,                   question
            (.)
```

Conversation Box 6.2
Extreme case formulations

In a classic study Anita Pomerantz (1986) showed the way that 'extreme' descriptions are commonly used where the speaker is resisting a complaint or similar. For example, when being questioned about why they have a gun in the house a caller to a suicide helpline claims that 'everybody does'. When the sales assistant is reluctant to give a refund on a pair of split shoes the customer describes them as 'brand new'. Note the extremity – it is not a lot of people who carry guns it is *everyone*; the shoes are not just new but *brand new*. People can formulate states of affairs in an extreme way to justify claims.

Derek Edwards (2000) has shown that speakers can use extreme case formulations, as they are hearably not literal, to display their *investment* in what they are saying. The following example is from a phone call where M develops a complaint about a Mrs Field using a long series of extreme case formulations, while L does only minimal agreements (the background is too complex to explain!).

```
M:      (A::susual.) If Louisa had (known) she wouldn't
        've uh (0.5) carted Missiz Field abou:t like she did (.)
ECF  →  all the time,
        (0.2)
L:      No:,
        (Edwards, 2000: 363)
```

M's use of extreme case formulations such as *all the time* displays her particular investment in the claim; L responds by distancing herself from it.

This analysis has implications for focus groups. We have noted that moderators often ask participants to avoid extreme constructions (see e.g. the extract on p. 93) and they may shift topic when extreme constructions are used (see e.g. extract on p. 129). Edwards' analysis provides a further way of understanding this. Extreme constructions display the speaker's particular investment in a claim about the product, and then this becomes a tricky environment for other participants to offer their views. It is notable that participants very commonly downgrade their formulations, as Stuart does:

```
I:: find it just a little bit. (.) yknow. >a bit< too big
(p. 130)
```

The downgrading counters any sense of investment in the claim, and therefore avoids trouble for participants offering different views. We can also see moderators picking this up in their glosses on participants' claims, as moderator Walter does in the following:

```
Okay, (.) so these first did well for (.) e:h (.) the reason
primarily >I guess< size. (.) A >little< more car like. Those who
have been saying is a little more compact (.) and, (.) got
versatility in here, to be able to fold down your seats
(p. 130)
```

Conversation Box 6.2   continued
Extreme case formulations

What we see with extreme case formulations, then, is the way descriptions of the world are crucially bound up with displays of psychology and have important consequences for how interaction unfolds.

Want to know more?

The original classic was Pomerantz (1986). Edwards (2000) has overviewed, updated and extended the treatment in important ways. His is a complex and intriguing article that repays repeated reading.

Mary	Powerful,	
	(.)	moderator looks round room
M: Brown	°Powerful,°	repeat receipt
Hannah	DOMIN↓ANT	
	(.)	
M: Brown	Dominant,	repeat receipt
	(1.4)	
Hannah	perhaps=a bit daring also,	smiles
M: Brown	Da-	starts to repeat
Hannah	Perhaps also, (.) because of the, (.) red ↑colour	
M: Brown	Hm mm,	
	(.)	
Hannah	Not too bour↑gois.	
	(.)	
→ Maria	Well I would rather have said, perhaps a bit con↑servative	conflicting description
	((soft laughter))	
M: Brown	((laughs))	
	(.)	
→ M: Brown	You said it too, right?	
Boris	Um mm.	
	(2.3)	
M: Brown	°Um mm,°	

Moderator Rich starts this extract with a projective question that requires brief descriptions as answers. He is asking participants to imagine the brand as a person and describe the characteristics of that person. This is not a question that is after POBAs, or elaborate descriptions or anecdotes. After Mary answers 'powerful' the moderator is immediately scanning the room, which he continues to do as he repeats the description. This both presents this brief descriptive answer as sufficient (he is not after any elaboration) and works to elicit further contributions. Hannah then provides another one-word description ('dominant') that gets a repeat receipt from moderator Brown.

Here we have the standard pattern:

Moderator	**Asks for description**
Participant 1	**Provides description**
Moderator	**Repeats key words**
Participant 2	**Provides description**
Moderator	**Repeats key words**

The moderator has successfully elicited answers that are *chipped in* by the participants. That is, they are not marked as agreeing or as disagreeing with the previous speaker, but are formulated simply as alternative characteristics. This is a key element to feature collecting. However, after moderator Brown has repeated Hannah's description, 'dominant', there is a longish pause. Hannah then comes in (her smile being an orientation to her deviation from the standard pattern) with a longer answer (note the way moderator Brown starts to repeat this but then breaks off).

When we consider the range of characteristics that have been provided at the start we can hear them as a relatively coherent list: powerful, dominant, a bit daring and not too bourgeois. What happens next is particularly interesting. Maria offers a description that clashes with the list. 'Conservative' and 'daring' could easily be heard as antonyms. Now note two things about it. First, Maria introduces this description cautiously:

```
Well I would rather have said. perhaps a bit con↑servative
```

There is a 'well' preface, and the description 'conservative' is hedged and softened ('rather', 'perhaps', 'a bit'). As we saw in Chapter 1, this is a classic feature of dispreferred seconds. What this shows is that Maria is having trouble chipping in here, she is orienting to the conflict between what she is claiming and what has previously been said. So we can see that the moderator has not been able to overcome the standard conversational organization of assessments and second assessments. The second thing to note is the moderator's receipt. Rather than do a repeat receipt, as he did with the earlier set of descriptions, he laughs softly. It is difficult to get the quality of this over in transcript; however, it does not sound hostile or critical. Rather, it recognizes how tricky it is to give a contrastive response. And he builds on this by addressing another participant, Boris, asking him to confirm that he had earlier made a similar contribution. So moderator Brown builds agreement between Maria and Boris rather than pursuing the conflict between Maria and Hannah. For example, what he does *not* do is ask the group: 'Which description fits better? If we think of the brand as a person is he daring or conservative?' That is, he steers the group away from arguing rather than towards it.

This leaves us with an interesting quality of feature collecting. Although it appears to allow variable descriptions that are just chipped in by participants, these descriptions often conflict with one another. They can appear contradictory in various ways – often through suggesting positive or negative assessments. Thus feature collecting is hard to keep insulated against the general conversational organization pattern where assessments tends to generate agreements. The bottom line, then, is that when moderators require more variation they need to steer their way around this organization. However, if they require more homogeneous descriptions then this organization can be exploited to deliver it.

SUMMARY

Focus groups are often used to identify a diversity of views. A range of different views can be used to help identify dimensions of an issue or product, and the different images people may have of it. Diversity will be more useful for some tasks than others.

Diversity is tricky. It can generate confusing variety and arguments between different group members. Conflict between group members can distort what is happening and make it hard to be clear about the different views that are held.

POBA talk invokes *multisubjectivity*. The very notion of an opinion or view has evolved for situations of difference between individual and groups. Nevertheless, diversity may be hard to generate with POBAs because of the strong everyday tendency in conversation to have an assessment of something followed by an agreement.

Moderators manage the issue of *variety* in their introductions in a number of ways.

- First, they may highlight the POBA idea that 'everyone has different views' and that variety is something desirable in the group.
- Second, they may stress that it is acceptable to disagree with other group members.
- Third, they may stress that they have no personal stake in the product – they will not be helped or made happy by purely positive responses.

Moderators manage the issue of conflict in a number of ways in their introductions.

- They stress the multisubjective feature of POBA talk that supports variety without disagreement.
- They downplay conflict, suggesting it is unlikely or trivial.
- They promote the idea of the group as collecting opinions that can be chipped in without having to develop or account for disagreements with others.

When participants start to disagree with one another, and this disagreement starts to descend into distracting argument moderators can do specific things to head it off. They often shift to a less troublesome topic, perhaps by asking a new question or reformulating the current question. Later, they can describe what went on in ways that avoid explicitly formulating the conflict.

Variety will arise across a group, and as different questions are asked. However, in any particular sequence of talk variability may be hampered by the tendency for people to provide agreeing second assessments. We discussed *feature collecting mode* as a technique for eliciting variety without argument. Feature collecting mode involves:

> **Moderator requests descriptions;**
> **Participant offers a description;**
> **Moderator does repeat receipt;**
> **Etc.**

Even here variety in responding is limited. Descriptions that are strongly contrasting or imply strongly different evaluations generate trouble. Moderators ignore such contributions or move things on by asking a new question.

TURNING PRACTICES INTO STRATEGIES

STRATEGY ONE
When you are starting the group, stress that people have different views and that it is helpful to express different views. You need to encourage an environment where people feel able to contribute without having to agree with what has already been said. It might be helpful to discourage participants from expressing views that are too extreme as it might restrict others' contributions.

STRATEGY TWO
Attend to your own position with respect to the product, service or policy. Stress your independence and your need for honest opinions rather than bland positive comments.

STRATEGY THREE
However much you have stressed that everyone will have different views it will be hard to counteract the general conversational expectation for assessments to be agreed with. Asking different versions of the same question may facilitate variety.

STRATEGY FOUR

Moving into feature collecting mode will allow you to collect a range of different descriptions. However, even here contrasting and contradictory descriptions will not be so easy for people to produce.

STRATEGY FIVE

If variation is essential, it may be highlighted at the report writing stage by checking through sequences dealing with different questions.

7 From Practice to Strategy

In this book our aim has been to highlight the basic skills that go into moderating focus groups. These skills may be taken for granted by experienced moderators; yet they can be particularly troublesome for novices. Part of the difficulty is that they come from a combination of explicit training and practical competence. The latter is much harder to formulate because it has been developed through a lifetime of interaction and has become so bedded in as to be invisible. Focus group moderation skills are to an important extent embellishments of everyday conversational skills.

We have tried throughout to examine closely the actual skills of actual moderators and use this examination to highlight some practices that are central to running a successful group. The theoretical and analytic perspectives of conversation analysis and discursive psychology have guided us in this. These have helped us focus the viewing lens onto what is important. The basic lesson is a simple one, however: that we should understand how to moderate focus groups by looking at what goes on in actual groups. This has led us to be wary of other kinds of writing on moderation that offers general normative lessons. These lessons may be useful, but their relation to actual focus group practice is a complex one. We have noted at various points how untrustworthy these lessons can be.

We have been cautious in offering strategies for moderation. We hope that our detailed examination of moderator practices may help moderators to examine their practices in a way that allows them to consider different options. As David Silverman (1997) suggests more generally for the application of conversation analysis, it may help practitioners better understand the intended and unintended consequences of their actions rather than offer fixed rules for success. It is for this reason that we have interspersed our text with boxes that note some of the more generic organizations of conversation.

Despite this, readers will have noticed that we have gone on to offer strategies. In the 'Turning practices into strategies' sections we have been unable to resist formulating general principles that moderators can put into practice. These principles are, more or less, developed out of our close analysis of the work of high-class moderators. Nevertheless, they are offered in a spirit which is somewhat playful or ironic. We hope that they may be useful – *aides-mémoire* perhaps, or a stimulus for thinking – but not taken as fixed rules.

The same might apply to the next section where we pick out and summarize some general themes that arise for the practice of moderation. The rest of the chapter will then be concerned with more speculative issues. We will ask whether the close examination of both interaction generally and interaction in focus groups specifically will allow us to suggest some deficiencies in current practice. More positively, and more speculatively we will end with some brief thoughts about the way focus groups might evolve in new ways that pay more account to modern thinking in conversation analysis and discursive psychology.

General themes in moderation – things that are *not* wanted

One simple way of considering the practice of moderation is as a way of facilitating interaction in the group that provides a lot of what you want, and not too much of what you do not want. We start with a consideration of some of the things that are not wanted on the principle of saving the best until last. It is not easy to be definitive because there are all kind of unexpected things that are not wanted (from participants turning up drunk to them dying in mid comment). However, the following things turn up so regularly that moderators will need some way of dealing with them. Doing this effectively will mark out a high class moderator. And, yes, we are offering some simple strategies. We have collected them together from the earlier chapters – but they should not be seen as a comprehensive list. Rather, they are indicative of what came before.

The participants play marketing expert, market research expert or social analyst

Participants play marketing expert when they start to make judgements about techniques of advertising or the reasons for presenting a service in a particular way. That is, they are acting as if they were the marketing experts judging image, audience, the effects of particular phrasing and so on. They play market research expert when they offer suggestions about what is going on in the group or how it might relate to findings or outcomes. They play social analyst when they offer judgements about 'what everyone thinks' or 'how young women all use shampoo', and so on. These are all activities that are unhelpful or even disruptive. The participants' role is to open up their lives for the research, not to theorize or speculate. The market researchers and product developers are paid to do this.

Head participants off by:

- setting out what *is* and *is not* required in the introduction;
- asking a new question;
- asking a new participant;
- asking a different kind of question.

All these strategies are indirect. They avoid telling participants that what they are doing is not what is wanted, which would probably discourage participation and highlight asymmetry between moderator and participant.

The participants tell personal anecdotes

People enjoy personal stories and may feel that such things are relevant to the research questions. Personal stories are sometimes interesting from a research point of view, and might be encouraged in certain specific circumstances (perhaps to find out experiences of what went wrong when using a new product). More often, they will disrupt the flow of the group, slow things down, and lead to large contributions from just a few individuals. Furthermore, as conversation analysts have observed (Jefferson, 1978), stories often lead to second stories and so on.

Head them off by:

- asking a new question;
- asking a new participant;
- asking a different kind of question;
- moving to a mode of questioning (such as feature collection) that requires brief answers broken up by moderator receipts.

Again these are indirect methods. Asking a group member directly to stop could be a delicate thing to do.

The participants generate account clutter

This is where participants provide contributions that are hedged around by account clutter: 'I am not sure, but'; 'I think, er, sort of, it is possible, sometimes that . . .'. Answers with a lot of account clutter are prefaced by, and threaded through with, expressions of uncertainty. This slows down the group by filling it with irrelevant material. It also makes the important things the participants have to say harder to pick out in between all the qualifications. In addition, it may indicate that participants have misunderstood the task. Account clutter can be generated where participants view the task as one of providing factual answers that can have correct or incorrect answers that they are not sure about. It may be exacerbated if the moderator is viewed as an expert on the factual topic.

Head this off by:

- emphasizing in the introduction that there are no right or wrong answers;
- stressing that responding will be quick and easy;
- generating informality;
- asking POBA questions where participants are unique experts on their own opinions.

These are mainly techniques for avoiding forms of responding that lead to account clutter. The presence of account clutter can be a useful diagnostic tool that the group has moved in an inappropriate direction. The exception will be in the (occasional) situation where members are asked factual questions to assess their knowledge of some product or policy.

Asking the moderator questions

Participants may ask the moderator about the nature of the product or policy, or about their personal opinion. These activities are potentially delicate because of their influence on the evolution of the group. If the moderator offers an opinion on a product it may be tricky for others to disagree. Asking the moderator about the product may be a consequence of the members viewing the moderator as a marketing expert (rather than a market *research* expert). Asking the moderator POBA questions may be a consequence of participants not being clear about the separate role of the moderator, seeing him or her as 'one of us'.

Head this off by:

- Showing group members that the moderator is not an expert on, or representative of, the product or policy. That can be emphasized in the introduction.
- Using a pattern of interaction that displays a neutral or disinterested position. This will involve a careful use of news receipts; for example, avoiding giving 'oh' receipts to participants' responses.
- Establishing a POBA focus. The beauty of POBAs is that participants are their own best experts on them; they should not need to ask the moderator.

Again, if the participants start asking the moderator questions this is a useful indicator that something has gone wrong with the set-up of the group.

Participants argue with one another

One of the features of getting a group of people together to provide their varied opinions on a product or policy is that it can turn into an argument. In a sense, the art of running a good focus group is keeping it hovering just on the edge of an argument – people are engaged, interested and offering their opinions in an animated manner – but it never arrives. It is a bit like surfing – you want to stay just on the wave without the wipe out.

Head arguments off by:

- emphasizing the legitimacy of members having their own views in the introduction;
- discouraging people from expressing strong or extreme views (these are hard to follow without explicitly orienting to disagreement);
- moving from POBA questions to descriptive questions;
- more generally, ask a new question, or participant, or type of question.

Arguments can slow things down and distort the whole trajectory of the group. However, they are a sign that the participants are highly involved in the group and, as such, a mixed blessing.

General themes in moderation – things that *are* wanted

What do you want from a market research focus group? There are only general lessons here, as different research topics and commissioning groups require different things. However, there are some general themes that we have been able to identify. In the language that we have been using a good group should provide the following things.

POBAs

These should be clearly and briefly expressed. Often moderators want them to be accompanied by reasons or justifications that are themselves clearly and briefly expressed. There should be some variation across the group. Whether this should include variation around a single theme or contradictory themes will depend on the broader aims of the group.

POBA talk is a wonderful interactional currency because it works in two directions at once. In one direction, it provides material that is ideal for policy makers, product developers, advertisers and politicians. It not only provides assessments of things, but the open-ended nature of focus group interaction (compared with a questionnaire or poll) allows members to select their own evaluative terms and dimensions. It can be so much more revealing to hear that a product is 'clunky' or 'old fashioned' than to simply register a tick next to the 'bad' or 'don't like' box. Moreover, the group does not merely provide the words in the report. Because of the use of the video and one-way mirror, it also provides vivid access to the *manner* of their delivery – its confidence, its emphasis, its coordination with the contributions of other group members and so on. This is what focus group workers mean when they talk about experiencing the experience of the members (Calder, 1977).

POBA talk is typically delivered with some justification, which may be quite minimal. Again this justificatory talk can be what is useful to product developers and others. It highlights just what is relevant for a positive or negative assessment. 'I wasn't so keen on that second vacuum cleaner, it's so old fashioned' is a statement that highlights the issue that needs attention. Note that these kinds of justifications are quite different from the sorts of account clutter that we have noted as a problem. Account clutter does not highlight what is relevant for the assessment; rather it provides general cautions about adequacy or truth of any claim. Mostly this is unhelpful and time consuming and groups should be organized to minimize its appearance.

POBA talk is not just important as part of the product of focus groups. POBA talk is equally important in another direction for its contribution to the flow of group interaction. POBA talk is pre-eminently talk in which the speaker is her or his best expert. You may not know the precise height of Mount Everest in metres. And if you claim it is a certain figure, someone can contradict you. Yet you know your own opinion that it is 'big', or 'striking' or 'that mountain that boringly obsesses people'. Someone might ask you *why* you think that, and might provide a justification for having a *different* opinion, but that is not to deny that *you* have that opinion.

Another feature of POBAs that is exploited in the organization of focus groups is that people are typically not expected to infer or work out their opinions or beliefs – they are immediate and available. This means that POBA talk can be quick talk. People asked about their opinions should have an answer at hand. Also, it is not easy to offer 'don't know' to POBA questions. Both of these are excellent qualities – they get things moving and make it easy to generate contributions from across the group.

Finally, POBA talk implicates variety. Opinions, beliefs and perspectives work within the logic of multisubjectivity. Different people may have different views. So POBA talk can support (a limited) variety compared with factual talk that assumes a single correct answer. All these features make POBA talk a central currency for focus groups. However, it is supplemented by talk in which participants offer descriptions.

Descriptive accounts

These too should be clearly and briefly expressed. Descriptions themselves often need no further justifications or reasons. Again there should be some variation across the group. The scope of the ideal variation will depend on the broader aims of the group.

One of the features of evaluations – the classic expression of attitudes and opinions – is as we have noted, that they get caught up in the conversational preference for agreement. People feel a pressure to agree with one another, and they find disagreeing tricky to do. A number of the moderator practices that we have discussed are meant to manage this problem. However, one powerful way around this is to ask questions that require group members to offer descriptions directly rather than yoking them to POBAs. Consider the following:

I love X shampoo, that bottle is so modern
subjective evaluation + descriptive account

Focus group moderators can use questions that separate out POBAs ('I love X shampoo') and descriptive accounts ('that bottle is so modern'), getting members to produce descriptive accounts without the evaluations. For example, projective questions and 'as-if' questions both head off the production of evaluations. It can seem like a rather odd thing to do – it is certainly one of the moderator practices that is less familiar outside of focus groups. However, the use of candidate answers and repeat receipts can facilitate the participants taking part in this practice effectively.

Descriptions are typically words or phrases concerning a product or policy. They capture and exemplify how the product is being viewed. Is it 'sporty' or 'smart' or 'stylish'? These categorizations may be just what is required to consider how the product will be marketed, who the consumers should be, or how it needs modification. Descriptions also do double duty in that they are *both* important group product *and* they contribute to the group interaction. First, they can be brief, often just one word is sufficient. This allows a lot of contributions from different group members in a short time. They do not require accounts, so this contributes to their speedy production. The moderator can easily regulate them by using repeats. In feature collection mode a limited variety can quickly be identified.

It is worth noting that things are a bit messier than this neat distinction between POBA questions and descriptive questions suggest. Our language provides the resources for keeping evaluations and descriptions separate. However, often the two things are collapsed together. Indeed, it can make sense in terms of conversational effort to have descriptions that work simultaneously as evaluations: try using 'dowdy' as a compliment or 'rich and varied' as a complaint (admittedly, with a bit of work it might be possible; conversation is pretty flexible after all!). However, the descriptive questions with moderator repeat receipts discourage the agreement organization that is pervasive with explicit evaluations.

In a typical focus group, of course, the moderator will ask a range of questions that require POBAs and others that require descriptions.

Questions, third turns and footing

Asking questions

To get the desired outcome from a focus group the crucial moderator activity is questioning. Questions necessarily manage a number of different issues at once and require considerable rhetorical finessing to get right. What is really tricky in focus groups is for the moderator to ask questions in a way that shows that she or he does not know the answer, but indicate the *kind* of answer that would be appropriate.

The centrepieces of focus groups are often elaborate questions requiring POBA answers. These questions are constructed around POBA terms – feelings, images, views, perceptions, opinions, attitudes and so on. These are the words that make the group members uniquely qualified to answer. Think of them as producing a universe where the participant is always right and the moderator never quite knows. This is a very reassuring universe for focus group members to work in.

Elaborate questions often start new topics. They do a lot of work shaping and guiding the answers. They include candidate formats for answering which nudge participants into a particular style of answering. And they often include candidate answers that display not only the style of answering but specific appropriate answers (brief, POBA based). These can be used to model how to answer. They guide participants, yet they do not close off novel responses.

If the work of the elaborate question has been successful they can be followed with minimal questions. These can simply elicit more responses (the ubiquitous 'what else?'), or ask new participants. At times follow-up questions can be used to elicit accounts for the offered answer ('why do you say that?').

We have distinguished POBA questions and descriptive questions. In practice they blur into one another. People can answer POBA questions with descriptions and vice versa. However, some questions specifically require descriptions. These are often organized in ways that ensure they will not be treated as factual questions. The classic form of this is the so-called projective question: 'Imagine the packets are people . . .'. This is

The basic 'adjacency pairs' identified by conversation analysts are question–answer, greeting–greeting, invitation–acceptance, and so on. However, Anita Pomerantz (1984) has studied the less familiar example of assessments. She notes that when one speaker makes an assessment of something the recipient is likely to make a 'second assessment' of their own. Here is an example:

```
J:      T's- tsuh beautiful day out isn't it?
L:      Yeh it's jus' gorgeous
        (Pomerantz, 1984: 59)
```

Second assessments (like L's 'Yeh it's jus' gorgeous') tend to be immediate and upgraded. It is easy to check this powerful organization for yourself. Just listen out for people making evaluations and listen for what comes next.

Indeed, you can see how strong this relationship is by looking at examples where the second assessment is absent. Speakers who withhold the second assessment are typically treated as disagreeing with the speaker rather than having no view. Again, this shows how powerful and psychologically inferential normative organizations like this are.

In conversational terms there is a 'preference for agreement'. This does not simply mean that people like agreeing (although they often do); rather, agreeing is both more common, and simpler to do. Disagreeing tends to be less common, delayed in the turn, downgraded or softened, and may be accompanied by an account. In fact, disagreements are very commonly prefaced by agreements. Look at the (familiar!) trouble in this exchange:

```
A:      Cause those things take working at.
        (2.0)
B:      (hhhh)
        well,
        They [do, but
A:           [They aren't accidents,
B:      No, they take working at, but on the other
        hand, some people are born with ((continues))
        (Pomerantz, 1984: 62)
```

Note the huge two-second delay after A's claim. B delays her answer even further with the long inbreath. She then prefaces her response with the token *well*. This is a very regular marker of something that goes against the standard preference organization going to happen. Then she prefaces her much deferred disagreement with an agreement (think how often we hear 'yes but' in this kind of situation).

Conversation Box 7.1   continued
Evaluations and their organization

The interest of this conversational organization for focus groups should be clear. The preference for agreeing with assessments is going to create a problem in a setting where a number of different speakers are providing assessments of some product. The preference will make it harder to disagree than agree, disagreements are likely to be rarer.

Want to know more?

The original Pomerantz (1984) paper is very clear.

projective because, classically, it is taken to be an opportunity for people to invest psychological desires and dynamics into the product. However, there is a variety of hypothetical or as-if questions that do much the same thing interactionally. These forms of question head off the possibility of a factual answer, and therefore the inhibiting possibility of being wrong.

There is a huge power in asking. Questions can set things, focus on particular words, manage asymmetry, change the subject, break up troubling interaction, select a new speaker, or display a playful, casual approach to the topic, and so on. They are fundamental to moderation. However, third turns are also important.

Third turns

In Chapter 1 we discussed the central conversation analytic observation, that much talk is organized in pairs of turns. And indeed much of our focus group material is organized into question–answer pairs. However, conversation analysts also emphasize the significance of the third turn. This can be crucial for the coordination of speakers or, as Emmanuel Schegloff (1992) puts it, their intersubjectivity. If someone invites you to dinner and you say you can make it at eight, and they then move to a new topic, have they understood? Are you going to dinner? Was your acceptance received? The 'third turn' is the place for receipt and clarification or repair – 'ok, got you', 'so that's eight this evening', or 'sorry, I meant next week'.

As we have seen, moderators use third turns to do a range of important things. The most fundamental is the repeat receipt, where words from the participant's answer are repeated. It is worth reviewing here the range of tasks that the repeat receipt performs, including:

- signalling the worthiness of the answer;
- showing attentiveness to answers;
- highlighting answers for viewers and video;

- modelling future answers;
- moving the question to a new recipient (when combined with gaze);
- avoiding showing moderator invention (which might suggest knowledgeability).

Footing

The sociologist Erving Goffman (1979) introduced the idea of *footing* to highlight the different conversational roles that people have in their talk. Rather than just speaker and listener, there are different speaking and listening roles. For example, people can be speaking their own words, characterizing the positions of others, or quoting what other people have said. Very different assumptions follow if you are giving your own view or reporting that of someone else. Likewise with listening. You can be the person being addressed, or you may be overhearing talk addressed to someone else. This is what Goffman meant when he said that people speak and listen on the basis of different footings.

The footing roles in a focus group are both complex and consequential. Moderators need to be a conduit to the clients, but not their representative. If they are treated as the client's representative this may encourage blandly positive responses. Moderators often make that separation clear, particularly when they are interested in critical or negative views. If the moderator is treated as personally interested in the product she or he may be treated as someone with expertise, and therefore asked questions. Moderators display themselves as experts on market research and what is going to happen in the group, but not expert on the product.

The participants also have an important footing position. In particular, they are encouraged to speak as unique experts in their own POBAs. At the same time, they are discouraged to speak as marketing experts, market research experts or as the relayer of the generalized views of other people.

For the moderator there is a tricky task of maintaining one's own footing position in the right area, and nudging the participants into the right position through the introduction, question construction and question receipts.

Big issues

For the rest of the chapter we consider some big, or at least troubling, issues. We consider: the idea of competence and training, issue of deceit, the role of traditional psychology, shortcomings in focus group practice and new market research possibilities.

Competence and training

One of the things that conversation analysts and discursive psychologists have done is show up the extraordinarily rich competence that people draw on in various everyday and institutional situations. Where traditional psychologists have often tried to highlight the limits or superficiality of everyday understanding, CA and DP workers have pointed to a complexity and sophistication that is often completely missed by researchers using traditional social science methods such as questionnaires or experiments. For example, if you are asked what you do when you go to the doctor you will probably give a rather superficial answer, which constructs what goes on in conventional or stereotypical ways. However, if we studied a video of your interaction it would reveal a complex pattern of joint, coordinated activity, with a range of very subtle cues being picked up and acted on.

This has implications for our own project in a number of ways. First, it cautions us to beware of accounts of focus group interaction from either members or the most experienced practitioners. It is simply hard to remember, capture, describe and communicate the delicacy of many focus group practices. They can be implied in general glosses but not easily described in their specifics. That is why we have based our suggestions on detailed analysis of video records of high quality focus groups.

Second, we are reluctant to make suggestions about the improvement of moderator practice. We have been continually impressed by the skills of the people we have studied and the effective way in which they coordinate the attention and contributions of a number of people who have never met on a topic that is probably new to them. Our approach has been to explicate this sophistication rather than to expect to improve it.

The third point is about training. In many ways a book is a rather ineffective training resource. Although it contains detailed records of focus group practices, these are in transcribed form, which is only partly able to capture the richness of the video records. Moreover, we have (sometimes against our better judgement!) ended up in making rather abstract, free-standing suggestions. At times we have suggested something a bit like rules for making moderation work. Our aim has been to be helpful but the limitations should not be underestimated. For this reason this chapter ends with some rather different strategic suggestions in the form of a practical exercise. This will take a bit of time, but will be most likely to improve practice.

The fourth and final point is about the quality of different moderators. It might seem that the stress on moderator skills being developments out of everyday skills means we are assuming that all moderators are equally competent. Are moderators always skilful, whatever they do? This is actually quite a complex issue. Conversation analysis highlights the systematic and coordinated property of interaction, and how it is designed to be learnable and usable by people with different knowledge and background (Schegloff, 1999). Conversation includes an emphasis on the display of sense as it goes along, and it provides various opportunities for repair of problems.

Nevertheless, the implication from this is not that everyone will be equally good as a focus group moderator. People can use the machinery and resources of conversation more or less well. We are all familiar with people who may seem boring, or self-obsessed, or inattentive or rude. These characteristics might all be cashed out in specific interactional limitations. Furthermore, it is not just a matter of doing everyday talk well; it is a matter of drawing on and developing its practices and doing a range of much more specialized questioning and receipting. Coordinating talk with six or eight other people at once is not everyone's strong point. It can involve a particularly active concentration on other people and what they are doing. It can also involve a confident ability to insert turns and, what we would loosely call, control the conversation. Like other things, people can be better or worse at it; and they can also improve with practice and training. We would like to think that this book will help people improve. Equally importantly, by spelling out what is involved in focus group moderation we can identify precisely what is involved in doing it badly.

Michael Bloor and colleagues (2001) retell an anecdote about a young moderator who was driven to tears by an unruly focus group, yet discovered all kinds of valuable material on the tape of the group. The moral they adduce from this story is that the moderator should not, and need not, try to control the group – good material will be generated whatever. This captures a certain truth about focus group interaction, and we too have argued against a simple idea of control. Nevertheless, the interactional procedures we have identified here are powerful and fundamental to how a group develops. A moderator with both a good intuitive feel for those procedures and a developed strategic grasp for them is in a good position to be able to manage what goes on and produce material that is coherent, visible and on topic.

Social psychology and psychoanalysis

The approach that we have taken to focus groups raises some interesting questions about the theoretical perspectives that are usually drawn on to make sense of what is going on in them. As we saw in Chapter 4, focus groups originated within a particular social psychology tradition, and the terms and approaches of that tradition are often used to gloss the way focus groups work. In addition, as we noted in our discussion of projective questions in Chapter 5, psychoanalysis has also been drawn on as a way of understanding how questions work and for interpreting results.

Traditional social psychology and psychoanalysis are both rich and complicated perspectives with much to offer human understanding. However, neither of them is focused on interaction; nor does either offer an effective apparatus for studying interaction. We noted that the notion of POBAs manages to provide a link to the traditional social psychology tradition while blurring things to an extent that allows moderators to not have to worry too much about the notion of attitudes. What we have done here is show up the way evaluations are developed in interaction, and some of the consequences that moderators need to attend to.

The broader question is whether the interpretation of focus groups and the understanding they generate should be cut loose from its social psychology history. We suggest that there is a case for considering focus groups using an interaction-focused treatment of evaluation. This would be useful primarily for helping to guide moderator practices. However, we suggest it might also be a more effective way of understanding the outcome of focus groups – the assessments, descriptions, claims and views that they offer.

The most radical version of the alternative view would be this. Talk about attitudes and opinions is a principal currency of focus groups not because it is the ideal coinage for market researchers, product developers and so on (although it is no doubt an excellent coinage for those users). Rather it is ideal currency because it is talk for which people have a *personal* speaking position. Indeed, they might be *expected* to have such a speaking position, and might be *accountable* for *not* having one. POBA talk is not so different from factual talk – it can take the form of a description of an object or policy, for example – but it does not require a right answer. Put schematically, it:

- should be easy to produce;
- does not easily fit the logic of 'don't knows';
- can legitimately vary between people;
- should not be already known by the moderator.

This will be an interesting theme to follow up in research. In our own work we have highlighted the way focus group moderator practices generate free-standing opinion-packages out of rhetorical and conversational patterns of evaluation (Puchta and Potter, 2002). However, there is still a lot to be done in the way of studies of evaluation in natural settings to help us understand what is going on here.

Our approach to psychoanalysis runs in parallel to our approach to traditional social psychology. Psychodynamic ideas have motivated various moderator practices. Most notably the practice of asking projective questions was developed with an explicit psychoanalytic gloss. However, we have suggested that projective questions may be useful in focus groups not

Conversation Box 7.2
Descriptions and evaluations

In our everyday interaction we offer judgements the whole time; we assess and evaluate things, or specifically hold off making evaluations, we compliment and complain. This is so important to human affairs that it is not surprising that there is such an elaborate and well developed set of resources for evaluation and such a varied set of evaluative practices. We have explicit evaluative words such as *like* and *love*, and they can be used in a way that attaches them to the speaker ('I love this shampoo') or to what is talked about ('the shampoo is lovely').

People do not have to use these evaluative words. They can describe things in many ways. Some of these ways can strongly suggest an evaluative stance on the speaker's part ('the pasta is too soft', 'the pasta is just soft enough'). Other ways of describing suggest neutrality or indifference. Studies of talk in the area of race, for example, have shown the way speakers can construct potentially racist evaluations as mere descriptions of how the world is. That is, they construct their descriptions as neutral or even anti-racist, but they are forced to recognize the way things are. A wide range of techniques is available for making descriptions seem more solid, objective and independent of the speaker's desires.

This complex arena is one of the areas of study of discursive psychologists. It addresses questions such as how psychological states are displayed and managed in talk. These phenomena are central to understanding what is going on in focus group interaction.

Want to know more?

For a summary of discursive psychological work on descriptions see Potter (1996). For a recent study of how evaluations are produced, and what they are produced *for*, see Wiggins and Potter (forthcoming).

---

so much because they can identify unconscious or hidden views, but because they are a beautiful pragmatic technique for generating a range of descriptions. Indeed, projective questions can be seen as part of a broader class of 'as-if' or imaginary questions that ask people to suspend factual criteria and in that way generate descriptions without the need for account clutter with less risk of deferring to the moderator as someone who knows best, and with less chance of a disagreement emerging between particip-ants. The general point, then, is that the usefulness of projective and similar questions may not be a product of an underlying theory of unconscious motivations but because they neatly circumvent the usual range of issues, problems and criteria that go along with factual talk.

These are complicated issues. In this context we are using them to raise questions rather than develop a full-scale alternative to traditional social psychology and psychoanalysis.

Deception

One of the themes in this book has been the complexity of operation of moderator practices and the way moderators deal with a range of dilemmas. For example, we have noted that a major issue is to guide the conduct of the group without appearing constraining or authoritarian. At times it may seem that what is being condoned or even encouraged is something that involves deception or manipulation.

Deception, manipulation and more general asymmetries in interaction are thorny issues. Take a visit to the doctor. Some traditional social researchers worried that doctors were browbeating patients with medical authority whenever they entered the surgery. However, careful studies of doctor–patient interaction highlight its closely collaborative organization, and the way that patients actively construct the medical authority and expertise of the doctor (Maynard, 1991; Silverman, 1987). Rather than see this as an imposition on the patient, we can see this as the collaborative construction of an effective service encounter. The patient is helping ensure that she or he gets expert judgements. None of this is to deny that doctors can be coercive or even abusive on occasions, or that they can mystify patients with medical expertise. Rather it is to note that the more familiar forms of medical interaction, which might appear coercive on the surface, have a more complex organization.

In terms of focus groups, we can consider the moderator practices of displaying informality, using candidate answers to guide responding, and so on as ways of enabling a particular style of interaction. They enable people to join in, be relaxed, be confident that they are providing what is hoped for (and what, typically, they are being paid for). Rather than considering it manipulative, it can be seen as a way of generating the interaction that provides an engrossing and relaxing experience with a light touch. That is not all that could be said on this tricky topic. However, we hope to have at least suggested a positive way to view these moderating practices.

Market research versus social science focus groups

One of the topics that has interested us when studying focus group moderation and in the writing of this book is the difference between market research focus groups and social science focus groups. Can we now give any better account of this difference? It is bound to be limited as we have not studied social science focus groups in detail and there is a range of differences within that category. Nevertheless, we have been able to draw on discussions of the nature of social science groups from Myers (1998) and Wilkinson (1998c). We have already noted some broad differences in the amount of interaction between group members that is encouraged and in the way the different styles of group are analysed. However, we are now in a position to highlight two more specific differences to do with the nature of market research *knowledge* and the different *footings* in the market research groups.

When market research focus groups are conducted the company or organization that commissioned the group is typically paying for three kinds of things.

- It is getting a report on the opinions, descriptions and so on of a set of people in relation to a particular object: an advert, say, or a new political policy.
- The organization is getting to view the interaction in real time through a one-way mirror.
- It is receiving a video record of the group that can be viewed and reviewed at will.

All of these things can input into marketing or product development. For example, if a political party is considering a new policy on health care, a focus group may highlight a range of concerns about the policy, things that are attractive, positive and negative descriptions and so on. These will appear in summary form in the report, and they can be accessed as part of the interaction through the mirror and on video. This will give a feeling for the vehemence of positions, the ease with which they can be produced in a group setting, and a host of things of this kind. These are not all easily formulated in abstract propositions. Yet they may be no less clear in a practical sense for all that.

This feature of market research focus groups has been emphasized in the idea that those who commission the group can 'experience the experiencing' of consumers (Calder, 1977). Most simply it is reflected in the common rationale that creative people offer for running and using groups. They want to hear consumers talk.

At the start of the book we emphasized how good people are at the practice of interaction, yet how relatively bad they are in describing or summarizing that practice. That is something that they do not have to do very often. Real life is, on the whole, a practical rather than theoretical enterprise. The use of market research focus groups draws on this practical skill. The viewers of the interaction do not have to have a precise technical language for everything that goes on for it to be useful and relevant to their job. Moderators help produce concentrated talk involving evaluations and descriptions that may be a practical guide to modifying an advert, considering dimensions of policy that might cause trouble, indicating hostility to an image.

In contrast to this, social science focus groups are typically used in relation to knowledge and theory (Kitzinger, 1994). These are abstract propositional things. That is, the findings often take the form of statements or propositions about the world – for example, 'radiation from nuclear reprocessing is a major danger in the environment'. To develop this relation focus groups need to produce things that can be spelled out in words, claims and arguments. This goes along with the publishing practice of social science. Social scientists do not typically get together to experience each other's research in any direct way. In social science, research is accessed through books and journals; that is, through media that depend almost exclusively on words and other formal representational media (numbers, diagrams and so on). Indeed, social science career paths depend on being able to publish in this form. Social science focus groups have to be run in a way that enables them to be transformed into a propositional form.

Some of the features of moderator practice we have identified in market research groups can be seen as ways of encouraging talk that is, relatively, direct and non-theoretical. Members are discouraged from playing market research experts, or sociological experts, in favour of offering POBAs and minimal justifications, along with simple descriptions. This fits with the use of focus groups as a medium for viewers to 'experience the experiencing' of consumers. What the group makes available is talk about products that is particularly rich in evaluation and construction – it provides judgements and categorizations, which suggest problems, delights, categories of users and so on. Furthermore, the risk when market research focus groups are turned into propositional output is that it will involve reconstructions in terms of traditional social psychological concepts such as attitudes or psychodynamic notions such as a projection. Market research focus groups have their own applied logic.

The second difference between market research and social science focus groups relates to issues of footing. As we noted above, the concept of footing highlights the different speaking and listening positions that are available in any interaction. We have already highlighted the way moderators encourage participants to take on certain footings and avoid others. However, there are also rather subtle differences in the listening footing. We touched on this earlier where we described the way moderators managed their stake and interest in the product by noting that they were not responsible for it, would not be upset if it was criticized and so on. Market research moderators build a footing that has them as a conduit to the company or organization that commissioned the group. This is somewhat analogous to the television news interviewer footing where they are asking questions on behalf of the audience (Clayman, 1992).

The key thing here is that the talk is produced with the company or organization as its explicit recipient. If you are in a group concerned with a shampoo advertisement you are likely to be told that the group has been commissioned by a particular company that wants to know how good the advert is. Your views have a specifically identified receiver. Even if no specific receiver is identified you will know that you have been recruited on the basis that this is market research being used by a company or organization.

In contrast to this, social science focus groups are likely to have been set up with an abstract footing. The research is not commissioned by an organization to check its advertising or whatever, but has been developed with abstract scientific goals. There is no clear final recipient of the talk. All kinds of people and groups could potentially be the recipients – some might like it, some might not. It will be interesting to explore the differences that this makes for the practices. For example, we can speculate that the market research pattern is closer to everyday evaluative talk where assessments can be used in a practical and communicative manner. The social science pattern is the more unusual as evaluations are requested with no clear recipient.

The complexity here is further increased because of the special recipient position of the other group members. This has been relatively under-theorized in work on focus groups. In what sense are the other group members recipients of talk? They are overhearers. But how far is the talk of any member fashioned, *recipient designed*, for other members? We can speculate that the increased inter-member interaction that has been noted as characteristic of social science over market research focus groups, combined with the lack of an identified recipient such as a company, leads to more of an emphasis on the other members.

Finally, it is worth noting a third common difference between social science and market research focus groups. In the former it is very common that the moderator is also the person who designs and executes the research and who writes it up. For this reason they often have a much stronger stake in the outcome than market research moderators. This may generate particular difficulties for moderator neutrality which are less apparent in market research groups. This can be roughly (and rather speculatively) summarised, as shown in Table 7.1.

Focus groups and the future of market research

Our approach in this book has been descriptive rather than critical. Rather than starting from the idea of what is wrong with focus groups and how they can be improved, we started by trying to see how they work. In particular, how can the particular practices that make up a good focus group be produced? How can moderators encourage what is needed and discourage what is not?

This approach is not a good basis for identifying problems and limitations with focus group research; nor is it intended to be that. Where we

Table 7.1   Differences between market research and social science groups

	Market research	Social science
Knowledge	Immediate Naïve POBAs + justifications Simple descriptions	Abstract talk Propositional talk Theoretical talk Arguments
Footing	Moderator = addressed recipient Members = overhearers Identified recipient = company/organization	Moderator = addressed recipient Members = addressed recipients, + overhearers No simple identified recipient
Stake	Moderator has little personal stake in expressed views	Moderator may have important stake in expressed views

have suggested problems this has been with the application of traditional social psychological or psychoanalytic stories to focus groups. Market researchers, political strategists and policy makers seem to find focus groups useful for their practices. We have concentrated on trying to show how that useful material is best produced. Nevertheless, at this stage in a book it is quite nice to let one's hair down and speculate a bit. So we end with brief thoughts on three issues: technology, new focus group practices, and the study of natural evaluations.

Technology

We have stressed that one of things that focus groups provide and marketers find useful is the possibility to view interaction, in their terms to *experience the experiencing* of actual consumers. Currently this is done overwhelmingly using the one-way mirror and videotape record. Let us consider the use of video. Videotape has the virtue of being cheap and familiar. Yet it is very clumsy to work with. It is slow to scroll through and hard to search for particular events (a particular question, say). It is also big and bulky and potentially fragile.

One concrete suggestion to make the group more useful would be to provide the video record in digital form on CD or DVD. A 90-minute focus group can be burned onto two CDs (or onto one DVD with plenty of space to spare). To make it convenient to use it could be burned into files that correspond to each new question or theme. The users could use these CDs or DVDs on their laptops or PCs. This has the enormous advantage of making the material immediately accessible. The market researcher can instantly access a particular topic on three different groups without scrolling through and ejecting tapes. The interaction can be viewed, frozen, slowed down and so on in a fluid and flexible way. Our suspicion is that the users of focus groups often do not use the video nearly as much as they might because of the practical obstacles that arise when using video. Anyone who has worked with digital materials in this way will wonder how they ever used VHS.

Modifying the group

The saying 'if it ain't broke don't fix it' seems well worth holding in mind here. However, if forced at gunpoint to suggest some ways in which focus groups might be developed, here are some thoughts based on our study of current group operation and our understanding of the general literature on interaction.

First, evaluations are practical. One of the observations highlighted in discursive psychology is that evaluations are used to do things – make compliments, request more food, turn down offers and so on. Can this practicality be captured more in a focus group setting? It suggests that there might be insight to be gained by trying to increase the participants' practical engagement with the product, even if it has to be role acting or imaginary uses.

Second, evaluations are accountable. Discursive psychologists and conversation analysts have emphasized the importance of uptake and accountability. Focus groups currently focus on evaluations and descriptions rather than their uptake. Might it be possible to combine the practical and accountable features of evaluations? What about exercises modelled on the following:

- Each of you should imagine you bought the product. Provide a simple justification of that purchase to the rest of the group. What would you say to boast about that product?
- Each of you should imagine that you were asked to buy that product by partner, spouse or friend. Provide a simple justification for not making the purchase. What would you say to disparage the product?

Or the possibility of rhetorical constructions could be explored.

- Describe the product in a way that emphasizes its qualities.
- Describe the product in a way that emphasizes what is bad about it.

Or for something engaging, but potentially hard to control: split the group into teams and have one team play sceptical and the other try to persuade them. Then turn this around; have one team play enthusiastic and the other try to dissuade them.

We have not evaluated these possibilities. They might generate more problems than they solve. However, they are offered to indicate how focus group research *might* develop to exploit the possibilities of interaction more fully.

Beyond the group

Some market researchers have begun to move beyond focus groups to do field observation and ethnography (Abrams, 2000; Desai, 2002). This is an interesting development and a development that has some affinities with the concerns we have raised about evaluations being practical and account-able. Everyday settings are the places where this practicality and account-ability is most apparent. There is a particular value to be had from being able to situate POBAs and accounts in their natural settings of use – in family homes, in shops, as partners argue about how to vote or how to spend their money. Such research is not without its problems, however.

In the first place, observations in the wild are only as good as the theoretical perspective that sustains them. If we expect such research to offer a direct pathway to such classic social science objects such as 'beliefs, attitudes and cultural values' (Desai, 2002: 15) then we are likely to get into a tangle. Currently this new style of work has not drawn on conversation analysis and discursive psychology, for example, and it tends to impressio-nistic and summary claims, even where careful video records have been made. The danger is that what is gained by the naturalistic setting is lost through reading into it a set of traditional social science or marketing categories.

In the second place, there are major problems of what social researchers call reactivity. This refers to the effects of recording on how people act. If research is going on involve film crews tramping around someone's house and researchers interviewing people as they live their lives this is clearly a source of distortion.

Despite problems of this kind, these approaches have huge potential. Reactivity can be managed by making the recording less intrusive (e.g. with fixed videos and radio mikes operated by the participants themselves) and by acclimatizing people to the research over a period of time. Material can be digitised and transcribed for careful study. Appropriate theoretical perspectives for natural interaction such as conversation analysis, rhetoric and discursive psychology can be drawn on to make sense of what is going on.

This will undoubtedly be an area of future growth. For the moment, market research focus groups are doing a job that has clearly not been surpassed.

Appendix: Transcription symbols used in this book

The standard transcription conventions for use in conversation analysis and discursive psychology were developed by Gail Jefferson. They emphasize things that are important for interaction rather than linguistics. They may seem a little unfamiliar at first, but their logic is straightforward. Most are simple developments from the normal symbols that are used in word processing. The main confusion is that the familiar punctuation marks are redefined to mark things about the way people talk rather than abstract features of grammar. So a full stop highlights a completing intonation – sometimes this will be at the end of a grammatical sentence, but not always. For more detail on transcription and the symbols used see the discussions in Hutchby and Wooffitt (1998) and ten Have (1999).

[ ]	Square brackets mark the start and end of overlapping speech. They are positioned where the overlap occurs, as shown below.
↑ ↓	Vertical arrows precede marked pitch movement, over and above normal rhythms of speech. They are for marked, hearably significant shifts.
Under<u>lini</u>ng	signals vocal emphasis; the extent of underlining within individual words locates emphasis, but also indicates how heavy it is.
CAPITALS	mark speech that is obviously louder than surrounding speech.
°practical°	'Degree' signs enclose obviously quieter speech (i.e., hearably produced-as quieter, not just someone distant).
(possible) (xxx)	Round brackets are used to indicate where the words are doubtful or a best guess. Where they cannot be guessed at they just enclose xxs.
(0.4)	Numbers in round brackets measure pauses in seconds (in this case, 4 tenths of a second). Place on new line if not assigned to a speaker.
(.)	A micropause, hearable but too short to measure.
she wa::nted	Colons show degrees of elongation of the prior sound; the more colons, the more elongation.

hhh	Aspiration (out-breaths); the more the longer.
.hhh	Inspiration (in-breaths); the more the longer.
Yeh,	The comma marks continuation, the speaker has not finished, intonationally it is a fall-rise or weak rising intonation.
y'know?	Question marks signal stronger, 'questioning' intonation, irrespective of grammar.
Yeh.	Periods (full stops) mark falling, stopping intonation ('final contour'), irrespective of grammar.
bu-u-	Hyphens mark a cut-off of the preceding sound.
>he said<	'greater than' and 'lesser than' signs enclose speeded-up talk. Sometimes used the other way round for slower talk.
Practical=what	'Equals' signs mark the immediate 'latching' of successive talk, whether of one or more speakers, with no interval. It can indicate that a speaker has 'rushed' to the next word in an utterance.
heh heh	Voiced laughter.
sto(h)p i(h)t	Laughter within speech is signalled by h's in round brackets.

The following passage has had the full range of transcription symbols added in to illustrate how they appear in actual transcript.

M: Yvonne	What do you think=what sort of wo:rds would you use to describe >if it was your< id_ea_l van. (.) yeah? (.) .hh and it was less, (.) less Noddy >like< if you like. (0.2) What sort of <u>words</u> would you use to describe the ideal= what [would it look] like
Graham	[Stylish]
M: Yvonne	Stylish, (1.0)
Diana	°Practical.°
M: Yvonne	Pra(h)ctical,=what else. (1.0) What would your ideal l<u>oo</u>k- look like. (1.0) °(say about you (0.2) >and< your company)°
Keith	A bit sporty?
Steve	SMA:RT

References

Abrams, B. (2000) *Observational research handbook: Understanding how consumers live with your product*. Chicago, IL: Contemporary Books.

Allport, G.W. (1935) Attitudes. In C. Murchison (ed.), *Handbook of social psychology*, Volume 2. Worcester, MA: Clark University Press.

Antaki, C. (1994) *Explaining and arguing: The social organization of accounts*. London and Beverly Hills, CA: Sage.

Antaki, C. (2000) Two rhetorical uses of the description 'chat'. *M/C: A Journal of Media and Culture*, 3. < http://www.api-network.com/mc/0008/uses.html >

Atkinson, J.M. (1982) Understanding formality: The categorization and production of 'formal' interaction. *The British Journal of Sociology*, 33, 86–117.

Atkinson, J.M. (1992) Displaying neutrality: Formal aspects of informal court proceedings. In P. Drew and J. Heritage (eds), *Talk at work: Interaction in institutional settings* (pp. 199–211). Cambridge: Cambridge University Press.

Atkinson, J.M. and Drew, P. (1979) *Order in court: The organization of verbal interaction in judicial settings*. London: Macmillan.

Axelrod, M.D. (1975) Marketers get an eyeful when focus groups expose products, ideas, images, ad copy, etc. to consumers. *Marketing News*, 28 February, 6–7.

Basch, C.E. (1987) Focus group interview: An underutilized research technique for improving theory and practice in health education. *Health Education Quarterly*, 14, 411–48.

Basch, C.E., DeCicco, I. and Malfetti, J. (1989) A focus group study on decision processes of young drivers: Reasons that may support a decision to drink and drive. *Health Education Quarterly*, 16, 389–96.

Bers, T.H. (1987) Exploring institutional images through focus group interviews. In R.S. Lay and J.J. Endo (eds), *Designing and using market research* (pp. 19–29). San Francisco, CA: Jossey-Bass.

Billig, M. (1988) The notion of prejudice: Some rhetorical and ideological aspects. *Text*, 8, 91–111.

Billig, M. (1991) *Ideologies and beliefs*. London: Sage.

Billig, M. (1996). *Arguing and thinking: A rhetorical approach to social psychology* (2nd edn). Cambridge: Cambridge University Press.

Bloor, M., Frankland, J., Thomas, M. and Robson, K. (2001) *Focus groups in social research*. London: Sage.

Branthwaite, A. and Lunn, T. (1985) Projective techniques in social and market research. In R.L. Walker (ed.), *Applied Qualitative Research* (pp. 101–21). London: Gower.

Brotherson, M.J. (1994) Interactive focus group interviewing: A qualitative research method in early intervention. *Topics in Early Childhood Special Education*, 14(1), 101–18.

Calder, B.J. (1977) Focus groups and the nature of qualitative marketing research. *Journal of Marketing Research*, 14, 353–64.

Calder, B.J. (1994) Qualitative Marketing Research. In R.P. Bagozzi (ed.), *Principles of marketing research* (pp. 50–72). Cambridge, MA: Basil Blackwell.

Catterall, M. and Maclaran, P. (1997) Focus group data and qualitative analysis programs: Coding the moving picture as well as the snapshots. *Sociological Research Online*, 2(1).

Clayman, S.E. (1992) Footing in the achievement of neutrality: The case of news-interview discourse. In P. Drew and J. Heritage (eds), *Talk at work: Interaction in institutional settings* (pp. 163–98). Cambridge: Cambridge University Press.

Clayman, S. and Heritage, J.C. (2002) *The news interview: Journalists and public figures on the air.* Cambridge: Cambridge University Press.

Coates, J. (1995) *Woman talk.* London: Routledge.

Cunningham-Burley, S., Kerr, A. and Pavis, S. (1999) Theorizing subjects and subject matter in focus group research. In R.S. Barbour and J. Kitzinger (eds), *Developing focus group research* (pp. 186–99). London: Sage.

Desai, P. (2002) *Methods beyond interviewing in qualitative market research.* London: Sage.

Edwards, D. (1997) *Discourse and cognition.* London and Beverly Hills, CA: Sage.

Edwards, D. (2000) Extreme case formulations: Softeners, investments and doing nonliteral. *Research on Language and Social Interaction,* 33, 347–73.

Edwards, D. and Mercer, N.M. (1987) *Common knowledge: The development of understanding in the classroom.* London: Routledge.

Edwards, D. and Potter, J. (1992) *Discursive psychology.* London: Sage.

Edwards, D. and Potter, J. (2001) Discursive psychology. In A.W. McHoul and M. Rapley (eds), *How to analyse talk in institutional settings: A casebook of methods* (pp. 12–24). London: Continuum International.

Folch-Lyon, E., Macorra, L. de la and Schearer, S.B. (1981) Focus group and survey research on family planning in Mexico. *Studies in Family Planning,* 12, 409–32.

Gardner, R. (1997) The conversation object mm: A weak and variable acknowledging token, *Research on Language and Social Interaction,* 30, 131–56.

Gardner, R. (2001) *When listeners talk: Response tokens and recipient stance, with special reference to 'mm'.* Amsterdam: Benjamins.

Glenn, P. (1995) Laughing *at* and laughing *with*: Negotiations of participant alignments through conversational laughter. In P. ten have and G. Psathas (eds) *Situated Order: Studies in the social organization of talk and embodied activities.* Washington DC: International Institute for Ethnomethodology and Conversation Analysis & University Press of America.

Goffman, E. (1979) Footing. *Semiotica,* 25, 1–29. (Reprinted in E. Goffman (1981) *Forms of talk.* Oxford: Basil Blackwell).

Greatbatch, D. (1986) Aspects of topical organization in news interviews: the use of agenda-shifting procedures by interviewees. *Media, Culture and Society,* 8, 44–56.

Goldman, A.E. and Schwartz McDonald, S. (1987) *The group depth interview: Principles and practice.* Englewood Cliffs, NJ: Prentice Hall.

Greenbaum, T.L. (1998) *The handbook for focus group research* (2nd edn). Thousand Oaks, CA: Sage.

Greenbaum, T.L. (2000) *Moderating focus groups: A practical guide for group facilitation.* Thousand Oaks, CA: Sage.

Henderson, N. (1991) The art of moderating: A blend of basic skills and qualities. *Quirk's Marketing Research Review,* December, 18,19,39.

Heritage, J.C. (1984a) *Garfinkel and ethnomethodology.* Cambridge: Polity Press.

Heritage, J.C. (1984b) A change-of-state token and aspects of its sequential placement. In J.M. Atkinson and J. Heritage (eds), *Structures of social action: Studies in conversation analysis* (pp. 299–346). Cambridge: Cambridge University Press.

Heritage, J.C. (1985) Analyzing news interviews: Aspects of the production of talk for an overhearing audience. In T.A. van Dijk (ed.), *Handbook of discourse analysis,* Volume 3 (pp. 95–119). London and New York: Academic Press.

Heritage, J.C. (1997) Conversation analysis and institutional talk: Analysing data. In D. Silverman (ed.), *Qualitative research, theory, method and practice* (pp. 161–82). London: Sage.

Heritage, J.C. and Greatbatch, D.L. (1986). Generating applause: A study of rhetoric and response at party political conferences. *American Journal of Sociology,* 92, 110–57.

Heritage, J.C. and Greatbatch, D. (1991) On the institutional character of institutional talk: The case of news interviews. In D. Boden and D.H. Zimmerman (eds), *Talk and social structure: Studies in ethnomethodology and conversation analysis* (pp. 93–137). Cambridge: Polity Press.

Heritage, J.C. and Watson, D.R. (1980) Aspects of the properties of formulations in natural conversations: Some instances analyzed. *Semiotica*, 30, 245–62.

Hutchby, I. and Wooffitt, R. (1998) *Conversation analysis: Principles, practices and applications*. Cambridge: Polity Press.

Jefferson, G. (1978) Sequential aspects of storytelling in conversation. In J. Schenkein (ed.), *Studies in the organization of conversational interaction* (pp. 219–45). London and New York: Academic Press.

Jefferson, G. (1987) Exposed and embedded correction in conversation. In G. Button and J.R.E. Lee (eds), *Talk and social organization* (pp. 86–100). Clevedon: Multilingual Matters.

Jefferson, G. (1990) List-construction as a task and resource. In G. Psathas (ed.), *Interactional Competence* (pp. 63–92). Washington, DC: University Press of America.

Jefferson, G., Sacks, H. and Schegloff, E.A. (1987) Notes on laughter in pursuit of intimacy. In G. Button and J.R.E. Lee (eds), *Talk and social organization* (pp. 152–205). Clevedon: Multilingual Matters.

Johnson, A. (1996) 'It's good to talk': The focus group and the sociological imagination. *The Sociological Review*, 44(3), 517–38.

Joseph, J.G., Emmons, C., Kessler, R.C., Wortmann, C.B., O'Brien, K., Hocker, W.T. and Schaefer, C. (1984) Coping with the threat of AIDS: An approach to psychosocial assessment. *American Psychologist*, 39(11), 1297–302.

Kitzinger, J. (1994) The methodology of focus groups: The importance of interaction between research participants. *Sociology of Health & Illness*, 16(1), 103–21.

Kline, A., Kline, E. and Oken, E. (1992) Minority women and sexual choice in the age of AIDS. *Social Science and Medicine*, 34(4), 447–57.

Knodel, J. (1995) Focus groups as a method for cross-cultural research in social gerontology. *Journal of Cross-Cultural Gerontology*, 10, 7–20.

Krueger, R.A. (1994) *Focus groups: A practical guide for applied research* (2nd edn). Thousand Oaks, CA: Sage.

Krueger, R.A. (1998) *Developing questions for focus groups* (Focus Group Kit, vol. 3). Thousand Oaks, CA: Sage.

Lunt, P. and Livingstone, S. (1996) Rethinking the focus group in media and communications research. *Journal of Communication*, 46(2), 79–98.

McQuarrie, E.F. (1996) *The market research toolbox: A concise guide for beginners*. Thousand Oaks, CA: Sage.

McQuarrie, E.F. and McIntyre, S.H. (1987) What focus groups can and cannot do: A reply to Seymour. *Journal of Product Innovation Management*, 4, 55–60.

Maynard, D.W. (1991) On the interactional and institutional bases of asymmetry in clinical discourse. *American Journal of Sociology*, 97, 448–95.

Merton, R.K., Fiske, M. and Kendall, P.L. (1990[1956]) *The focused interview: A manual of problems and procedures*. Glencoe, IL: Free Press.

Morgan, D.L. (ed.)(1993) *Successful focus groups: Advancing the state of the art*. Newbury Park, CA: Sage.

Morgan, D.L. (1997) *Focus groups as qualitative research* (2nd edn). Thousand Oaks, CA: Sage.

Morgan, D.L. (1998) *The focus group guidebook* (Focus Group Kit, vol.1). Thousand Oaks, CA: Sage.

Morgan, D.L. and Krueger, R.A. (1993) When to use focus groups and why. In D.L. Morgan (ed.), *Successful focus groups: Advancing the state of the art* (pp. 3–19). Newbury Park, CA: Sage.

Myers, G. (1998) Displaying opinions: Topics and disagreement in focus groups. *Language in Society*, 27(1), 85–111.

Padilla, R.V. (1993) Using dialogical research methods in group interviews. In D.L. Morgan (ed.), *Successful focus groups: Advancing the state of the art.* Newbury Park, CA: Sage, 153–66.

Peräkylä, A. (1995) *AIDS counselling: Institutional interaction and clinical practice.* Cambridge: Cambridge University Press.

Philo, G., Secker, J., Platt, S., Henderson, L., McLaughlin, G. and Burnside, J. (1994) The impact of the mass media on public images of mental illness: Media content and audiences belief. *Health Education Journal,* 53, 271–81.

Pollner, M. (1987) *Mundane reason: Reality in everyday and sociological discourse.* Cambridge: Cambridge University Press.

Pomerantz, A. (1980) Telling my side: 'Limited access' as a 'fishing' device. *Sociological Inquiry,* 50, 186–98.

Pomerantz, A. (1984) Agreeing and disagreeing with assessments: Some features of preferred/dispreferred turn shapes. In J.M. Atkinson and J.C. Heritage (eds), *Structures of social action: Studies in conversation analysis* (pp. 57–101). Cambridge: Cambridge University Press.

Pomerantz, A. (1986) Extreme case formulations: A way of legitimizing claims, *Human Studies,* 9, 219–29.

Pomerantz, A. (1988) Offering a candidate answer: An information seeking strategy. *Communication Monographs,* 55, 360–73.

Potter, J. (1996) *Representing reality: Discourse, rhetoric and social construction.* London: Sage.

Potter, J. (1998a) Discursive social psychology: From attitudes to evaluations. *European Review of Social Psychology,* 9, 233–66.

Potter, J. (1998b) Cognition as context (whose cognition?). *Research on Language and Social Interaction,* 31, 29–44.

Potter, J. and Wetherell, M. (1987) *Discourse and social psychology: Beyond attitudes and behaviour.* London: Sage.

Puchta, C. and Potter, J. (1999) Asking elaborate questions: Focus groups and the management of spontaneity. *Journal of Sociolinguistics,* 3, 314–35.

Puchta, C. and Potter, J. (2002) Manufacturing individual opinions: Market research focus groups and the discursive psychology of attitudes. *British Journal of Social Psychology,* 41, 345–63.

Richter, M., Bottenberg, D. and Roberto, K.D. (1991) Focus groups: Implications for program evaluation of mental health services. *Journal of Mental Health Administration,* 18, 148–53.

Sacks, H. (1992) *Lectures on Conversation,* Volumes 1 and 2, ed. G. Jefferson. Oxford: Basil Blackwell.

Sacks, H., Schegloff, E.A. and Jefferson, G. (1974) A simplest systematics for the organization of turn-taking for conversation. *Language,* 50 (4), 696–735. (Reprinted in J. Schenkein (ed.) (1978) *Studies in the organization of conversational interaction* (pp. 7–55). New York: Academic Press.)

Schegloff, E.A. (1968) Sequencing in conversational openings. *American Anthropologist,* 70, 1075–95.

Schegloff, E.A. (1992) Repair after next turn: The last structurally provided defense of inter-subjectivity in conversation. *American Journal of Sociology,* 98, 1295–1345.

Schegloff, E.A. (1995) Discourse as an interactional achievement III: The omnirelevance of action. *Research on Language and Social Interaction,* 28, 185–211.

Schegloff, E.A. (1999) Discourse, pragmatics, conversation, analysis. *Discourse Studies* 1: 405–13.

Silverman, D. (1987) *Communication and medical practice: Social relations in the clinic.* London: Sage.

Silverman, D. (1997) *Discourses of counselling: HIV counselling as social interaction.* London: Sage.

Stewart, D.W. and Shamdasani, P.N. (1990) *Focus groups: Theory and practice.* Newbury Park, CA: Sage.

ten Have, P. (1999) *Doing conversation analysis.* London: Sage.

Vaughn, S., Schumm, J.S. and Sinagub, J. (1996) *Focus group interviews in education and psychology*. Thousand Oaks, CA: Sage.

Wiggins, S. (2002) Talking with your mouth full: Gustatory mmms and the embodiment of pleasure. *Research on Language and Social Interaction*, 35, 311–336.

Wiggins, S. and Potter, J. (forthcoming) Attitudes and evaluative practices: Category vs. item and subjective vs. objective constructions in everyday food assessments. *British Journal of Social Psychology*.

Wilkinson, S. (1998a) Focus groups in health research: Exploring the meanings of health and illness. *Journal of Health Psychology*, 3(3), 323–42.

Wilkinson, S. (1998b) Focus group methodology: A review. *International Journal of Social Research Methodology*, 1(3), 181–203.

Wilkinson, S. (1998c) Focus groups in feminist research: Power, interaction, and the co-construction of meaning. *Women's Studies International Forum*, 21(1), 111–25.

Wilkinson, S. (1999) How useful are focus groups in feminist research? In R.S. Barbour and J. Kitzinger (eds), *Developing focus group research* (pp. 64–78). London: Sage.

Wooffitt, R. (1992) *Telling tales of the unexpected: The organization of factual discourse*. London: Harvester/Wheatsheaf.

Wooffitt, R. (2001) Researching psychic practitioners: Conversation analysis. In M. Wetherell, S. Taylor and S.J. Yates (eds), *Discourse as data: A guide for analysis* (pp. 49–92). London: Sage.

Zanna, M.P. and Rempel, J.K. (1988) Attitudes: A new look at an old concept. In D. Bar-Tal and A.W. Kruglanski (eds), *The Social Psychology of Knowledge* (pp. 315–34). Cambridge: Cambridge University Press.

Index